GOING OUT

ON TOP

THE EASY-TO-UNDERSTAND GUIDE
**FOR A HAPPY, HEALTHY,
PROSPEROUS RETIREMENT**

GOING OUT

ON TOP

DAVID J. KATS, D.C.

LEVI

Publisher's Cataloging-in-Publication Data
(Provided by Quality Books, Inc.)

Kats, David J.
    Going out on top : the easy-to-understand guide for a
happy, healthy, prosperous retirement / by David J. Kats
— 1st ed.
    p. cm.
    ISBN: 0-9701782-1-2

    1. Retirement. 1. Title.

HQ1062.K38 2001   646.7'9
                            QBI01-200028

Library of Congress Catalog Number: 00-112265

ISBN: 0-9701782-1-2

Printed in the United States of America

First Edition

ACKNOWLEDGEMENTS

A book of this kind could not be written without the contributions of numerous people. I have woven their ideas together, but without these individuals there would be no book.

For contributing their time and their expertise, I wish to thank attorneys Gary Lodmell, Douglass Lodmell and Don Bowman. I would also like to thank Dr. George Rejda for his input and critical analysis.

Thank you to Marilyn Beyer for her hours of meticulous proofing and editing of the manuscript.

Debra Butcher also deserves an expression of gratitude for agreeing to be project manager and for guiding the project from beginning to end.

FOREWORD

Some people never have the opportunity to retire, other people just once, and a few have the opportunity to retire twice. Dave Kats may be one of the fortunate ones – he may retire twice.

At age 37 Dave Kats sold his chiropractic practice — one of the largest in the United States — and retired. Within months he realized that while he was financially able to retire he was not psychologically ready to retire.

His hobby, working as a business consultant to other chiropractors, soon became his full-time occupation — and passion. Kats Management, the consulting firm he started, is now the nation's largest chiropractic consultancy. Kats Management consultants now work daily with chiropractors and other health care professionals in various stages of their journey toward retirement. Building the practice, reducing debt, creating savings programs, and investing properly are all part of the plan.

Dr. Kats still isn't psychologically ready to retire — according to him, he may never be. He loves his consulting and speaking opportunities. His book on retirement is one of the best to guide you through your journey — simply written to provide a strong foundation for a great retirement.

Keith Maule
Kats Management, CEO

TABLE OF

CONTENTS

INTRODUCTION

I t's March 29, 1982. A crowd of 61,000 people is gathered in the Superdome in New Orleans. There are 17 seconds left to play. What happens in those 17 seconds determines who will be the NCAA National Basketball Champions. The Georgetown Hoyas have been a perennial powerhouse, but the University of North Carolina is in the hunt for their first National Championship. The ball moves to the hands of a North Carolina freshman, who rises up among the rest, and confidently fires a 17-foot jump shot, comes down and waits for the sweet sound of the net. The rest is history.

To this day Michael Jordan still calls this shot the most important one of his career. For basketball fans it was the shot that was heard around the world. A shot that would over the next two decades bring basketball to a new prominence and make the name Michael Jordan a household word. That was 1982 and the University of North Carolina, via Michael Jordan, went out on top.

The year is 1998. The team is the Chicago Bulls. There are 5.2 seconds left on the clock. The National Championship hangs in the balance. Michael Jordan has already come out of retirement once, and many feel this will be his last game. Michael takes the ball. He moves quickly to the right, sheds a defender, and rises up among them. It's another jump shot. As the ball leaves his hand, his arm is extended, his wrist is limp, and his fingers relaxed. There's that sound again — the net. The Chicago Bulls are National Champions. It was the last shot Michael Jordan ever took in professional basketball.

Michael isn't the only person that finished with a burst. In 1941 Ted Williams was batting .404. It was the last game of the season. According to various reports, the coach gave Ted the opportunity to sit the game out. Doing *so would ensure his .404 batting average for the season — and for history. If Ted did play and was unable to get a hit, it was possible that his batting average would drop below .400 — and the record he prized most would evaporate. He made the decision to play, went 2 for 3 in the game, and ended the season with a .406 batting average — a feat never again accomplished in baseball.*

It seems that some people have a natural ability to go out at the top of their game. That's what this book is about, looking into your future and making the right decisions — allowing you to go out on top.

RETIREMENT: THE LAND OF OPPORTUNITY

Today we live in the land of opportunity. Our generation will live longer than any other generation before it and have a greater chance of maintaining good health later into life than our parents or our grandparents could ever have dreamed. Today we are seeing hoards of baby boomers enter retirement, and starting now and for the next twenty years we will be seeing huge changes and opportunities for retirees. We will have the opportunities to travel, learn, work, play, create, start new businesses, and almost anything else we desire. The changes are already starting to take place. There are senior citizen discount travel programs; schools and colleges are offering reduced or free tuition for seniors; job fairs are recruiting the recent retiree; and entire communities, who once shunned retirees, are now recruiting them aggressively. We are starting to see retirement communities — not nursing homes but actual retirement communities — where we can live and have fun together! We are indeed very fortunate. The flip side to this opportunity is responsibility. We are ultimately responsible for the happiness, health, and prosperity we attain in retirement.

Today there are an estimated 30 million retired Americans and another 15 million Americans with more than $500,000 in assets who are approaching retirement age. With impending retirement moving closer at such a rapid rate, it would seem that everyone would be interested in planning their retirement future. Yet studies show that only one half of American workers between 30 and 50 years old have analyzed their retirement needs. The others continue to run toward retirement blindfolded.

Planning ahead is important. According to the Benefit Research Institute, of the people who have analyzed their retirement needs, 88% say they are setting money aside compared to only 61% of those who have not analyzed their retirement needs. It clearly helps to have a goal.

WHAT ARE YOU GOING TO DO IN RETIREMENT?

If you are reading this book, you are probably thinking about retirement. What are your goals? How do you see yourself spending your retirement years? It used to be simple — the rules were clear — you worked 30 to 50 years for the "company," got your gold watch, pension, Social Security, and sat down on the front porch to watch the cars go by and wait for your children to come over and visit. But retirement isn't that simple anymore — and that's good. Today retirement can be almost anything you want it to be. Since people are retiring younger, they have an opportunity to do things their parents could not. They're active enough for athletic competition and young enough to travel, get a degree, do volunteer work, or even launch an exciting new career.

However, amidst this optimism we must be careful. There are some traps which can create major problems: inflation, taxes, lingering debt, underestimating life expectancy, being taken advantage of financially, thinking that Social Security will take care of you, and failing to get the rest of the family involved in your retirement. There is also the unpredictable — you or your spouse could become disabled, you could have a boomerang child (one that comes back to the nest after once being independent), you may have a need for drugs not covered by Medicare or lack health insurance if you retire before you are 65 and are not Medicare eligible.

It will be a great journey, but we must climb with care and confidence.

RETIREMENT INFORMATION

Why do accountants, certified financial planners, or other financial authorities write the books on retirement? Why don't medical doctors write books on retirement? Isn't good health one of the most important aspects of the retirement years? How about alternative health care providers, like chiropractors? They deal with the aging population and pioneered the wellness concept. Or, how about ministers, rabbis, priests, or even psychologists? Isn't spiritual and psychological well-being one of the most important factors in retirement? Isn't depression a common ailment found in many retirees?

Here's the answer: The most frequently asked question about retirement (although not necessarily the most important) is — will I have enough money to retire? As a result, we see lots of books on retirement, but they are really only books on the financial aspect of retirement. The last printed material I reviewed was entitled *The Ultimate Retirement Guide, Answers to All Your Questions*. On the cover are listed the following subtitles:

1. Stocks
2. Funds
3. IRAs
4. 401(k)s
5. Annuities
6. Withdrawals
7. Rollovers
8. Insurance
9. Real Estate
10. Taxes
11. Online Tools, and more.

If this is the *ultimate* retirement guide, with answers to all your questions, what happened to discussing issues of family, health, retirement dream homes, and leisure time?

Perhaps the only people qualified to talk about retirement are retired people! They can teach from experience. To them, only the final chapter is a mystery. In my last years of high school, it became apparent that our school was so small it would be consolidated with other schools in the area. This would involve relocation of the school. When it passed by a vote of the people, many of the career teachers left for teaching jobs with a more certain future. As a result, there was a scramble for teachers to fill one-year teaching positions. The shortage grew so severe that the school board resorted to hiring a 72-year-old principal out of retirement. The shortage also caused him to take on teaching responsibilities. And as luck would have it, I had him in two classes — Geometry and World History. Geometry was a disaster. While I suppose squares and circles have been around for a long time, their understanding had evaded him. World History was quite a different story. We were studying about France in the First World War. I vividly remember in class one day when we were about six weeks into the school year and sixty pages into the text book, he looked up at the class, closed his book and said, "You won't need to refer to the text book anymore. The rest of this book isn't history to me. It's current events!" Mr. Schneider, our teacher, suddenly became the most interesting and informative teacher we could have ever had. Reason: He had lived through it. Maybe only retirees should write books on retirement! Art Linkletter said, "Kids and senior citizens are the only people that tell the truth. Kids don't know any better and old people don't care anymore. Their friends are all dead anyway."

Some retirement books are also written by people who have a hidden agenda. If the author sells a product such as insurance, retirement planning services, or retirement community real estate, it's easy to get a jaded picture of what you truly need for retirement. Now don't get me wrong, many of these books have wonderful information, but remember that you may have to temper it with other information to complete your total retirement plan. *Going Out On Top* gives you an impartial look at all aspects of retirement.

GATHERING INFORMATION

For the past 20 years I have worked as a consultant to professionals, which has afforded me the opportunity to deal with the retirement issue on a continual basis. When I decided to put the concepts, thoughts, and ideas that we use with our retirees into print, I realized I needed to get a more well-rounded approach regarding how people view retirement. This was done through surveys and focus groups.

I started by sending a survey to 1,000 professionals and executives. Two hundred thirty-three responded. The survey and its results are found in Appendix B. I then held several focus groups, which included doctors, millionaire executives and professionals, a random selection of retirees, and a random sampling of the employed population. The surveys and focus groups were done in an informal way and probably would not stand up to the scrutiny of professional analysis but they gave enough additional information to make the book complete. Since I work predominantly with chiropractors and other health care professionals, this book leans slightly more toward the retirement of professional or executive level people, but the concepts will be valuable for anyone who is considering retirement. Finally, I used the world's most modern clipping service, the Internet, to fill in the holes and provide statistics.

Throughout the book I have used some averages and assumptions — a practice warned against by many financial planners. I, too, realize that the indiscriminate use of assumptions and averages can be misleading. We've all heard the illustration of the man who had one foot in hot water and the other foot in ice water. On the average, the temperature was just right. By the same token, we cannot treat the future as a precise science. For example, just a few years ago financial planners advised against working in the retirement years, because Uncle Sam would take back one dollar for every three you earned; but since the beginning of this decade that is no longer true. And who can predict just what your tax rate will be when you start using your tax-deferred retirement accounts? Predicting the future is not a precise science. Just as space ships need minor corrections as they travel their course, retirement plans need flexibility to accommodate future change.

This book wasn't written to be "The Last Retirement Planning Guide You'll Ever Need." It was written as a primer — a book that you'll understand, a book that will help you create the right attitude toward retirement, a book that is not intimidating, and a book that will act as a springboard for more in-depth study if you desire. The good news is this: The mere act of planning your retirement has the effect of increasing the savings of those who take time to do it.

WHAT'S AHEAD — *A Sneak Preview*

Some parts of this book are more fun to read than others. We like to think about leisure time, travel, and vacation homes, but aren't quite excited about insurance, taxes, and long-term nursing home care. However, to maintain a well-rounded perspective on retirement we need to cover all facets of retirement. The chapters on insurance and investing are written in simple language and intended to give an overview that will help you in working with your personal advisors. Even if you don't understand everything discussed in the chapters on insurance and finances, don't get discouraged. Since the chapters do not build on each other, the next chapter is filled with easy-to-understand information.

Chapter 1 — Permission to Retire

It sounds crazy, but some of us actually need permission to retire. Although many of us have an honorable goal of retiring early, the actual act of early retirement sometimes causes consternation with friends, family, and the retiree himself. This can lead to indecision, procrastination, depression, family stress, and living a life you're not interested in living (working after you feel like you have the right to retire). Once you feel you've "earned the right" to retire, your retirement planning becomes much more effective.

Chapter 2 — Your Attitude Toward Retirement

Your attitude toward retirement varies greatly depending on how your retirement happens. If you are forced out of work or forced into retirement, you may have a negative attitude. On the other hand, if you've completed a lifetime project, or sold your company for a handsome profit, you may have a much more positive perspective. As a practicing chiropractor in the late '70s, I treated a man named Al who worked at a rubber factory. For the last five years before retirement he could hardly move his legs. As he sat on a chair in the treatment room, legs extended, he would place his hands under the back of his leg and lift his leg, which would allow him to pull his feet closer to him. He would tell stories of how he was mistreated at work and couldn't wait to retire. Soon after he retired I noticed that his visits became much less frequent, and when he did come in, he had a spring in his step I hadn't seen for years. For him, retirement meant breaking the 40-year shackles of a distasteful job. But Al isn't typical. More than likely your attitude in retirement will be similar to your attitude before retirement. If you're happy while working, you'll most likely be happy in retirement. You see, happiness is not a "where or when," it's a "here and now." If you can't be happy where you're at right now, it will be difficult to be happy in retirement.

Chapter 3 — How Soon Can I Retire?

How soon do you want to retire? One comedian joked that he wanted to live long enough to be a burden to his kids. But when you think about it, that's probably not a very exciting thought for either him or his children. Outliving your money is perhaps the single greatest concern of the retiree. Volumes are written about the subject, often with such complicated terms and worksheets that they make the IRS long form a pleasant experience. I recently talked to a soon-to-be-retired gentleman that had a doctor's degree. After completing one of the worksheets on retirement found in a financial periodical, he called and said, "Either I calculated wrong, or I can't retire until 3048."

There are two ways to decide on your retirement date. The first is to calculate the amount of money you will need in retirement, calculate your current savings rate, and then determine how long it will be until you have reached the "magic number" and can retire. The other way is to decide on a logical retirement date and adjust your savings plan so you reach your desired goal on or before the day you want to retire. We'll discuss both.

Chapter 4 — How Much Money Do I Need?

Wow, that's a loaded question! Ask fifty financial consultants how much you need to retire and you will probably receive fifty different answers. That's true in part because we are attempting to predict the future. No one knows exactly what the inflation rate will be or what type of return you will get on your retirement savings. We can, however, make some fairly safe assumptions and come up with a fairly accurate plan that allows for your cost of living, normal inflation, typical return on investment, and life expectancy.

Your financial retirement plan does not have to be complicated. Chapter 4 lays out the basics in easy-to-understand scenarios.

Chapter 5 — If You Still Have Time to Save

A few years ago I was in a hotel room watching the *Oprah Winfrey Show*. Her guest was Mark Levine, co-author of *Live Rich and Die Broke*. They had opened the program to questions from the audience. One lady stood up and said that she had spent much of her earlier life supporting her children and then in later life helping with the care of her mother. She had nothing set aside in savings and casually mentioned that she felt it was about time to start thinking about putting some retirement money away. The author asked her age, to which she responded 59½ years old!

I hope you haven't waited until 59½ to start a savings account for retirement! If you have, you will find your back is pretty much against the wall. Unfortunately, most of us have probably waited a little longer than we should have to start saving for a retirement. Today, according to the Public Agenda Foundation, 46% of Americans, including people age 51-61, have less than $10,000 saved for retirement, and an AARP study shows the typical baby boomer has only $1,000 in assets! But if you still have ten years left, you're not totally against the wall. You still have some wiggle room.

Chapter 6 — *Partial Retirement vs. Full Retirement*

There are as many ways to retire as there are people retiring, so we will just cover the major retirement opportunities. Many people want to work part-time during their retirement. They even look forward to it — and not just people who need the money. Remember, during his first retirement, Michael Jordan worked as a baseball player, and during his second retirement he is active in basketball management.

There are some wonderful opportunities in part-time retirement. You can start a new career, work a flexible schedule, work at your leisure, take long vacations, and still manage to work in retirement. As late as the mid-1990s, only 28% of men and 18% of women ages 65-69 were still working, but according to the American Association of Retired Persons (AARP), more than three fourths of the baby boomers expect to retire at age 65. And of those people, three out of four expect to continue working at least on a part-time basis. On the other hand if your idea of retirement is sitting out on a boat in the middle of the ocean, you have that opportunity, too.

Chapter 7 — *Social Security*

Some say Social Security is here to stay, and others say it is almost gone. Who's right? Today our benefits from Social Security look healthier than at any time in the recent past. This is due in part to budget surplus and in part to the rules that went into effect January 1, 2000, that did away with the financial penalties for working in retirement and allow you to keep Social Security benefits regardless of the amount you earn.

Chapter 8 — *Investing For The Future*

This chapter won't intimidate you. The chapter is filled with easy-to-understand ideas and concepts to help you invest while in retirement. While it is very important to understand the basics of retirement investing, you will still need a good retirement attorney, accountant, financial planner, and other advisors. They are the experts, but you will still need to know enough to make good investment decisions.

Chapter 9 — Where Are You Going to Retire?

There are many books that list the most popular retirement spots in the United States and they're great for reference. But even the most beautiful setting, climate, education, and cultural opportunities may pale in comparison to the first time you hold your new grandbaby in your arms. Being close to that grandbaby is enough to make you move from Maui to Davenport, Iowa! In other words, the "human" factor will play a large part in deciding where to retire. Once those human elements are factored in, the other criteria like climate, cultural events, natural beauty, and ease of travel, can be considered.

In past years, as many as 83% of the people over fifty said they would like to retire in their current home. But more recent studies suggest that younger Americans are more likely to want a new environment for their retirement years. This is true in part because our society has become more mobile and in part because we are retiring younger and have the opportunity to enjoy a more transient lifestyle. Today about one third of Americans ages 40-54 expect to move when they retire and 39% of 25-39-year-olds expect to move when they reach retirement age. Whether you plan to move or stay put, you need to have a plan.

Chapter 10 — What Will the Kids and Spouse Say?

One of the consultants in our management firm lives in La Jolla, California. He loves the area and frequently spends time on the beach with his wife. But the biggest local attraction for this California couple is their grandchildren who live just a few miles away. Recently they thought their son's job transfer might cause the grandchildren to live in Omaha, Nebraska. As nice as the beach is, they were willing to move to Omaha just to be with the grandkids! It's surprising what kids (and grandkids) will do to your thoughts of retirement. And what if your spouse has a different retirement plan than you do? It is difficult to live happily-ever-after in two different states!

Many of us think about helping our children during the early years of retirement, but in later years it is very possible that our children may be helping us. My mother was able to spend the last five years of her life in her own home, even though she was on oxygen 24 hours per day and was somewhat unstable when walking. She would never have been able to maintain a private residence had it not been for the fact that my three sisters and I took turns visiting her for a few hours each day. Your retirement plan isn't just YOUR retirement plan; it also involves the rest of the family.

Chapter 11 — Your Home or Homes

What will your retirement home really look like? You may respond, "I'm already living in it." Many people have no plans to leave their current home. On the other hand, some people dream of moving to a new home when they retire — possibly even a new state or country! So, whether you're thinking about moving to a different country, or just what to do when your kids come home, the home you have in retirement becomes important. If you're too frugal you may soon feel cramped. If you overspend to build your dream home, you must realize that every dollar spent on a home is a dollar not invested in your retirement account.

Chapter 12 — Your Mission

For many people retirement is the first time they can seriously work on what they consider their real mission in life. Their past job was mediocre at best, and instead of working on *their* goals, they were forced to work on "company" goals. But now it's time to concentrate full-time on your own goals, your mission — your passions! Without goals and a mission your retirement may seem dull and undirected. But if you are finally on track to fulfill your mission, retirement can be tremendously exciting!

Chapter 13 — Health and Wellness

Surf's up, Gramps! That's the title of an article in the recent *Business Week Magazine.* The article says, "As baby boomers turn 55, they will be more active and healthy than any preceding group of that age. More and more seniors are shunning golf clubs and walking shoes for hardier sports, from heli-skiing to surfing, and even triathlons. These very active over 55ers say that participating in sports that sparks an adrenaline rush keeps them physically fit and makes them mentally younger, too."

While you may not be the tri-athlete type, you still have an obligation and opportunity to lead a healthy life and participate in the wellness programs springing up for retirees throughout the country. Retirement is a good time to put off old bad habits and take on new good habits. Proper exercise, eating, and sleeping can improve your retirement years. You don't want to act like your parents during their retirement years, do you? You're younger, healthier and stronger! In fact, last year, the retirement community of Sun City, Texas published *Aged Beef: Men in their Prime*, a calendar featuring pin up shots of male residents. Sales were so brisk that publishers couldn't keep it on the shelf. This year Sun City plans a version featuring women, and with participation in demanding sports on the rise, there ought to be plenty of models to choose from. The challenge will be getting them to hold still.

Physical and mental health are two of your greatest retirement assets. Protect those assets.

Chapter 14 — Your Hobbies

During the focus groups we found that many people who are within ten years of retirement reported that they had no hobbies. When questioned more closely, we found many actually had hobbies they enjoyed but had not developed because of the lack of time. If you're planning to retire in the next few years, you should start developing your hobbies now. Don't worry about what other people think of your hobbies. They're yours! If you like to do them, who cares what people think? One focus group participant said she couldn't wait to retire so she could concentrate on politics. Yuck! I'm thinking about hiring an illegal immigrant just so I'm never tempted to run for Vice President!

We found that most people had "undeveloped" hobbies — things they love to do but had never cultivated. If you search hard enough, you'll probably find that you do have various hobbies. I have five. I enjoy running, collecting Indian artifacts, paleontology, singing, and travel. My wife is a pilot and enjoys flying, volunteering for a prayer line and other church activities, and surfing the net. We both like to take various education classes. I fully anticipate that we will complete additional degrees after we retire.

Chapter 15 — Insurance

Let's face it, some chapters are more exciting than others! Most people don't find insurance too interesting. And to make it worse, we expect that our cost of insurance will increase as we age. There is, however, some good news. Some insurance premiums may go away, including disability insurance payments and health insurance payments.

While insurance isn't the most exciting thing to think about while preparing for retirement, it is absolutely necessary. We'll do a quick overview of how to get the most from your insurance dollar spent, and make sure there are no holes in your insurance plan.

Chapter 16 — Asset Protection

Here's a sad thought: If you're entering retirement, you probably now have more money than you will ever have again! For many, retirement marks that point where saving stops and spending starts. There are, of course, some exceptions. If you've tucked away so much for retirement that you cannot spend all the interest, you may be piling that interest back into your retirement account. But, for most people, their net worth at retirement is at an all-time high, especially considering adjustments for future inflation.

Because most of us will not earn significant amounts of money in the future, we must be extra careful with the money we have now. This means more than just investing it wisely. We must also continue to protect our assets against lawsuits, judgments, and disreputable people eager to take the retiree's fortune. Recently, a grandmother found that she was liable for damages incurred when her grandson had an auto accident with *his own car*. The courts ruled that since the grandmother loaned her grandson money to buy a "high performance" car, she should be held liable for his inability to control that car and causing an accident. We'll discuss various levels of protections ranging from simply putting your money in low risk investments to forming international asset protection Trusts.

Chapter 17 — Passing Your Assets On

Recently, I saw a cartoon of two old men sitting on a bench outside a country store engaged in leisurely conversation. The caption underneath read, "I didn't want to marry her for her money, but it was the only way I could think to get it."

You will pass your assets on. The question is to whom, and how efficiently you will pass them. Estate taxes can take a major bite out of your assets. Wills, Trusts, and other legal documents can be difficult for older people to understand and should be in place well before your retirement years. Planning ahead can save thousands of dollars.

Passing your assets on includes more than just finding legal ways to give your money to your heirs. You have more than financial assets. You need to consider how to pass on other things including your values, spiritual beliefs, and the ability to accumulate money for retirement. If there's ever a time you want to "teach a man to fish," it will probably be in retirement.

Chapter 18 — Staying Happy Throughout Retirement

"And they lived happily-ever-after" is easier said than done.

Depression is a real factor to deal with in retirement. It comes both from the fear of the unknown and through natural body changes as we age. But it does not have to be an inevitable part of retirement. Retirement can be a mountaintop to mountaintop experience if we create and work the proper retirement plan.

Well-planned retirement provides so much opportunity. Just like Michael and Ted, we can go out on top!

PERMISSION TO RETIRE

T en years ago a young man contacted our company. He had just graduated from chiropractic college and was returning to the Midwest to set up his practice. As with many young graduates, he was eager to get into practice, and he built his business fairly rapidly. After a few years in practice he had become very successful and already had a practice that was more profitable than the national average. During one of our consultations this young bachelor told us that he had met a girl and was quite smitten with her.

A few months later, I talked with him again, and it seemed he was still quite interested in her. It looked like a marriage might be in the making.

At our next consulting session he mentioned not only that they were talking about marriage, but that he had met her mother and father and she seemed to come from a fairly well-to-do family. Six months later they were married. But, the big surprise came when he told me they had recently inherited a portion of the family's wealth, and the taxes on their portion alone were over twenty million dollars!

Now, I know what you're thinking — he married for money! But the truth of the matter is, he knew nothing about her money until he was madly in love with her! And it couldn't have happened to a nicer guy. They have a beautiful marriage and wonderful kids. His wife spends most of her time in low-profile philanthropic activities.

Now here's the interesting part — his most recent calls to our office were to seek guidance about retirement. He had practiced only for about ten years *and would probably have practiced another 10 or 20 years had it not been for the inheritance. Eventually, it boiled down to this: He felt guilty retiring so quickly after all the time, effort, and money he had put into his education and practice. In some way, his upbringing made him feel guilty about leaving his chosen profession. After several discussions he decided his responsibility of helping manage the family's finances was more important than keeping his practice. He sold his practice a few months later.*

WHAT ARE YOU WAITING FOR?

Ah...Retirement. What a wonderful thing! Sleep in as late as you want! And you never have to go to work again! You are now joining the ranks of the fastest-growing segment of the American population. In 1940 there were only 123,000 Americans age 65 or older. Today there are 30 million such Americans. It is estimated that in 2050, there will be 50 million Americans over the age of 65. Add to that the number of Americans that will be retiring before 65 and the ranks swell to 70 million — over one fourth of the United States population today.

Now, if retiring is so wonderful, why is it that I don't feel quite right about doing it — in fact I feel a little guilty? That's a common question among potential retirees. Perhaps the biggest reason is the fact that retirement is so final. As teachers, we let our teaching certificates lapse; as physicians, we place our licenses on inactive or let them lapse; and as factory workers, we realize there is very little chance to go back once someone else has been trained to take our place. This means all of our calculations had better be correct. If we outlive the money we now have, finding more will be very difficult.

Then there's the American work ethic. All of our life we've worked 40 hours a week, sometimes more. Normal, respectable people work! Now, if we retire, especially if we retire early, many of our friends and colleagues who are the same age as we are will continue to go to work every day. And since we're able-bodied, just like everyone else, somehow it just doesn't seem quite fair. In addition, some professionals feel they have had a "special calling." If God calls a minister into the ministry, does He call him out at some time, too? Or as a minister, am I just greedy if I want to retire early? Did I lose my first love for the profession?

Well, here's the answer: There's nothing wrong with retiring early, especially if you've done the math and other soft calculations and are sure that you are financially and psychologically ready for retirement. In truth, many of us can do more for our families, our community, and ourselves in retirement than we can working our 40 hours-a-week job.

It's time we stop worrying about what people think. After all, you are retirement age — you're old enough to make your own decisions. It's time to stop doing what your parents want you to do!

Doesn't it seem ironic that for years we dream of early retirement — and it's even considered noble to have an early retirement goal — and now that we stand on the threshold of opportunity, we seem unwilling to grab the brass ring. I say seize the day! It will give you the opportunity to do all the things you want while you're still young and able to enjoy them.

Now that you've given yourself permission to retire, you may still be looking for permission from a few other sources, like your profession, your family, and your friends. As far as your profession is concerned, it can probably survive without you! A standup comic once said, "Don't take yourself too seriously, just remember when everything is said and done, the number of people that attend your funeral will probably be predicated on the weather that day!"

Your spouse and family are a different story. You will want their approval *for* retirement as well as their input *about* your retirement. You've heard all the stories of the working man and stay-at-home wife. The man retires and is underfoot all day long. He is finally happy, but the wife is driven to distraction! Sharing your retirement dreams, goals, and challenges with your spouse and family early in the planning process will help meld ideas, create clearer visions, and produce less friction.

Why not take your spouse on a weekend retreat with the agreement that you'll spend quality time together talking about your future retirement plans. With time set aside for this open, candid discussion, you and your spouse will become more comfortable with the idea of retire-ment. Some of the questions will start to be answered, and you will begin to visualize the good life of retirement. Once you reach this point, your need for "permission to retire" will be met.

2

ATTITUDE
TOWARD RETIREMENT

One extremely hot summer day, while on break from chiropractic college, I found myself back on the farm helping my dad haul hay. I was in my late twenties, which put him in his late fifties. If you've never lived on a farm, you can't imagine the work involved with hauling hay. The bales are heavy, the sun is scorching, and every time you lift a bail over your head, dry alfalfa leaves stick to the sweat on your face and arms, and fall down the front and back of your shirt. I had just arrived at the age where I realized that my father was indeed getting older. This was hard work for him. Because I loved him, I wanted to go the extra mile to help him out.

When you store hay in a barn, you work in one of two positions. You either work outside placing the bales of hay on an elevator, or you work inside a hot, dark hayloft (storage area), where the elevator drops the bales and all the loose alfalfa leaves which creates a terrible dust. Since I felt twenty and Dad looked sixty, I decided I would take the toughest position — in the hayloft. For the first thirty minutes things worked just fine, then it seemed like the bales kept coming faster and faster. I suddenly realized that I had been a professional student for the last six years and he had been a farmer! After that came a second realization — before starting to unload the next wagon, the kindest thing I could do for my father was to take the outside position, because if I didn't, he would have to dig his 29-year-old son from under a pile of a thousand bales at the end of the day!

That's just the way he was. Nearly a workaholic. Working fast and steady, all day long, six days a week, every day of his life. He was a great husband and father, but when it came to farming, it was all work, dawn to dusk.

Eventually he retired, sold his farm equipment, and moved to town. They say you can take the boy out of the country, but you can never take the country out of the boy. There are a few exceptions, and my father was one of them. Most retired farmers can tell you the price of wheat or hogs twenty years after they retire. Dad wasn't one of them. Within two years after he retired, in small talk one day I asked him what the price of wheat was and how many bushels per acre farmers in his area were receiving from the harvest. He had no idea! From the day he sold his farm equipment and moved to town, he never looked back. Later in his retirement, I asked him if he missed farming. He said, "Not really. I looked forward to retirement for so long that I don't feel the need to look back." Even though my dad had worked fulltime on the farm from the time he was pulled out of school after six weeks in the ninth grade until he was 67, he had managed to create an attitude which let him enjoy his retirement years.

HOW DO YOU SEE RETIREMENT?

How do you view retirement? As with any change in life, you have to be emotionally ready for retirement; you have to address the psychological aspect of retiring. If you're looking forward to retirement and anticipate it as a welcome change in life, a new adventure, then you will probably find it to be so. By the same token, if you consider retirement a necessary evil, something you don't really want but are forced to do, you might find your worst fears confirmed. Henry Ford said, "Whether you believe you can, or whether you believe you can't, you're probably right."

Retirement is not the end of the road — it's a curve in the road. There is still more living ahead. With a good attitude you'll enjoy your work, work hard, make a lot of money, and retire sooner. With a bad attitude you may get fired, bounced around from job to job, and never retire. A good attitude makes retirement a blessing; a bad attitude makes it depressing.

Perhaps the most important message in this book is that you are retiring "to something" and not just retiring from a job. Retirement is not "doing nothing." The more you prepare for those exciting years, the more fulfilling they will be. You will probably become in your retirement what you picture right now. If you change the picture, you will be able to change your retirement outcome.

EMOTIONAL ISSUES

Financial Stress

During the second half of 1987 interest rates in the United States rose and the bond market declined. The world's most sophisticated stock investors panicked, sending the stock market down 30% or more. Meanwhile, real estate markets in the United States were plummeting because of overbuilding, new tax legislation, and rising interest rates. Oil and gas prices dropped because of an oversupply. It was a dismal time for investors living off their assets.

The fear of financial loss or inadequacy is one of the most prevalent emotional issues to deal with in retirement. In the years before retirement, every time a few thousand dollars were added to the retirement account, there was a heightened sense of financial security. But in retirement, any decline in total investment value because of low returns or excess spending can send people into a deep depression. Uncontrolled, this concern can ruin their lives. A few retirees might even commit suicide.

Ed was one of my high school football coaches. He was credited with turning around the football program. I also had him as an instructor for a few classes. He had a tremendous command of the English language, great reasoning skills, and a deep throaty laugh that made you feel good all over. He was also a pillar of the community, serving on many different boards including the State Parole Board. About ten years after high school graduation I was devastated to hear that Ed had placed a gun in his mouth and committed suicide. I understand that after retirement some of his investments had turned bad, and he became severely depressed.

While most of us certainly wouldn't react that way, you can be assured that your financial fears will not end with retirement. Every year that you withdraw money from your retirement fund and all the markets you are in decline, you'll assume the worst and calculate how few years you can live on your retirement nest egg if it continues to decline at its current rate.

The good news is markets virtually never continue to decline! In fact, we are living in one of the biggest bull runs in history and many sophisticated market analysts, such as Harry S. Dent, author of *The Roaring 2000's*, feel very confident that the market will continue its rapid growth for the rest of this decade.

The Fear of Growing Old

When we first think of retirement we tend to think short-term. We look for retirement homes near beaches, not hospitals; we value homes because they are near the airport instead of because they are barrier-free. While it's natural to think about the good times that will happen early in our retirement years, it's obvious that retirement marks the last third of our life...which ends with our death. And while it's good to plan for the end of our life, there's no reason to obsess about it. It all boils down to the question of how you see the glass. Is it half empty or half full? In today's society, retirement is too long to not live it to the fullest. Socrates said the unexamined life is not worth living.

Psychologists suggest that the way to overcome fear is by creating an even more powerful desire. Fear of the stage is overcome by a stronger desire to perform. Fear of a skiing mishap is overcome by desire for the excitement of the downhill slope. Your fears of various negative retirement issues can be overcome by anticipating the joys that retirement brings. A clear vision of retirement can help create the desire which overcomes fears. Figure 2.1 provides an exercise that can help you create a clearer retirement vision. You may want to take time to clarify your retirement vision before moving on.

FIG. 2.1

RETIREMENT VISION

1. *What are the three best things about my retirement?*

2. *Who do I know that is retired and 65 or older that I admire?*

3. *How have they handled their retirement?*

4. *What responsibilities will end when I reach retirement?*

5. *What opportunities will I have in retirement that I do not have now?*

6. *How will retirement improve my family life?*

7. *How will retirement improve my spiritual life?*

8. *How will retirement improve my physical life?*

9. *How will retirement improve my educational life?*

10. *What will I do with my leisure time?*

3
HOW SOON CAN YOU RETIRE?

Moving is a terrible job. All the decisions regarding what to pack, the packing itself, heavy lifting, unpacking, and then more decisions about where to place things in your new house can be mind-boggling. Moving a large office is even harder. About two years ago we were moving our main office from one 6,000 square-foot building to another. After we had completed most of the packing, professional movers arrived with their trucks, ramps, and dollies. It was a typical moving crew, lots of young, strong guys — except for one who was a man in his fifties. As the day wore on I was surprised how well he was able to keep pace with other younger, stronger bodies around him. On the second day my curiosity got the best of me, and I asked him how long he had been in the moving business. "Only a few years," was his reply, "but I'll probably be doing it for a long time. See I took my retirement right out of high school! I figured I'd retire while I was young and could enjoy it, so now I'm paying the price. It was a fine party! It lasted for about 25 years. So, I suppose I'll be working into my eighties."

YOUR RETIREMENT PHILOSOPHY

While I'm not comfortable with the previous philosophy, it does have a thread of logic in that, to a certain extent, we can select our retirement date. He was simply subscribing to George Bernard Shaw's philosophy when he said, "It's too bad that youth is wasted on the young!"

When are you going to retire? If I asked you to state the year of your retirement out loud right now, could you do it? Have you even narrowed it down to the closest year? If not, now's the time to start planning. There are two ways to look at when you can retire. The first way is to use financial calculations (which you will do in Chapter 4) and the second way is through the setting of a personal goal.

Using the financial procedure you simply ask: How much will I need to retire? How much have I saved to date? How much am I now saving on a regular basis? What is my estimated return on investment (ROI)? And, finally, when will I amass enough that I can live on those investments? After making the calculations, you will arrive at your date of retirement. And while this may be an over-simplistic view of financial planning for retirement, it is the essence of how many people calculate their retirement age.

On the other hand, some people who are more goal-oriented use this approach: When would I like to retire? Then, how much will I need to live on? How much do I have in savings right now? What will be my return on investment? And then, how much will I need to save per year to retire "on time?"

Question: Which is the best approach? Answer: Neither is the best approach. The best way to set your retirement date is by blending the two ideas. The financially-oriented approach lays out a logical plan. The goal-oriented approach ties that plan to a specific timeline. A goal without a plan is just a dream. A plan without a timeline runs a high risk of never being executed. People that have goals, but no plan, will dream of a financially secure retirement, but may never reach it. People who understand the plan, but have no timeline to create urgency, may find that their retirement date and the second date on their tombstone coincide!

WHEN ARE PEOPLE RETIRING NOW?

It's amazing how many people automatically tie their retirement date to their eligibility for Social Security retirement. Is that always logical? A story was told of a young man who was impatiently waiting for his wife to make some last-minute dinner preparations before they left for church. As he walked into the kitchen she was cutting the end off a roast before cooking it. When he asked why she was doing that, she said, "We've always done it that way." When he pressed her as to "why" she informed him that it was the way her mother had always done it, and if he was so interested in "why" he could ask her mother when they got to church. After the church service, the family gathered at the mother's home. The young husband proceeded to ask the mother why she cut the end off the roast. She replied, "We've always done it that way. It's just the way Grandma used to do it." When he pressed her as to "why" she said, "I suppose you'll have to ask Grandma." Soon Grandma arrived and the family sat down for the meal. At the family table the roast was served. As it was being served the young man said to the grandmother, "Why do all three of you cut the end off your roast before you cook it?" To which she responded, "I've never had a roasting pan, and the roast won't fit in a regular pan unless I cut off the end. I have no idea why my daughter and granddaughter continue to cut the end off the roast!"

In large part, I believe that's why so many Americans feel they should retire at age 65. A few generations ago, times were tough. You had to work until 65 — your life expectancy was only 68! Social Security was a big portion of your retirement plan. If you were going to retire, 65 was the magic number.

That's not true any longer. Today, we are seeing retirement ages that range from young to very old. Many professionals are retiring at younger ages. According to the American Medical News, physicians are now entering into early retirement because they're frustrated by managed care regulations and bolstered by a strong stock market. In a telephone survey of 300 physicians that were fifty years old or older, they found that 38% plan to retire in the next one to three years, 68% plan to reduce their work load, 12% will work as temporaries, 10% plan to see no patients — and in fact, change their career — and only 18%, less than 1 in 5, plan to continue as usual. Even though 60% of the doctors claim their single biggest source of satisfaction comes from patient relations, 10% say they plan to seek employment in a "no clinical" setting. In fact, the average age of the retiring physician dropped from 69.8 years in 1980 to 67.4 years in 1995. During that same time, the average retirement age for all American workers dropped to 62 from 64. One doctor said, "We see a push out factor in dissatisfaction and a pull out factor from having a strong stock market in the recent past, creating more assets."

In the American society today, we see an increasing division between the haves and have-nots. One segment of the American society is doing better, saving more, and just plain getting ahead. The other segment seems to be bogged down in high consumer debt, underemployment, and virtually no savings. I predict that as this population ages into retirement (which is occurring right now) you will see that same dichotomy appear. Many people, having planned properly, will retire early and into a life of financial freedom and personal leisure. They will see significant fulfillment of their goals, dreams, and ambitions well into their retirement years. Some, probably many, will continue to work part-time, but only to maintain well-roundedness, high self esteem, and to give back to the community. On the other hand, the have-nots will be divided between those people who continue to work beyond typical retirement years out of financial necessity and those who will consign themselves to living a lifestyle that Social Security benefits and meager personal assets will afford them.

HOW LONG WILL YOU LIVE?

How long will we live in retirement? The amount of money we need for retirement is relative to how long we will live during our retirement. In financial planning for retirement, if you are going to err, it's best to err on the side of financial security! While the average American's life expectancy has now risen to 76 years, we have to realize that this figure takes into account everyone who has died before age 65. The fact is that for every year you survive, your life expectancy increases. A man who has reached the age of 65 can expect to live another 15 years. But to be on the safe side, a 65-year-old should plan on living another 30 years. This means when we "choose" a life expectancy somewhere between 90 and 95 years, it is a pretty safe bet.

LIFESTYLE IN RETIREMENT

Most authorities agree that the average person will spend less in retirement that they did before retiring. This decrease in spending is somewhat natural. You will no longer pay for disability insurance, you may have need for fewer cars, you may downsize your home, and your wardrobe will include fewer work clothes. You will also have more time to do projects that you may now pay for, and with the increased possibility of no children at home and no full-time job there will be less wear and tear on your house, car, and other major assets.

This type of decrease is good and leads to a natural question. Should we plan on decreasing our lifestyle even more now so that we can retire earlier? There is an ever-increasing group of people who longs for retirement but has not saved appropriately. So, the concept of leading a simple retirement lifestyle in an effort to retire early (or on time) can be appealing. But be careful not to plan on cutting back on your lifestyle too drastically. While it may sound good, we must realize that we have some long-practiced habits. Whether these include church giving, eating out, cable channels, newspaper subscriptions, or alcohol consumption, your habits are fairly well established. If you try to cut down drastically, you may find that diets lead to binges. There's a saying that for every diet there's an equal and opposite binge. This is because the forced diet causes a sense of deprivation that is frequently remedied by overindulging. This cyclic approach in retirement can cause great consternation, depression, and fear. There's really no point in giving up your job two years early just to live a deprived lifestyle for the next thirty years. There are better solutions.

ADVANTAGES OF EARLY RETIREMENT

All things considered, a majority of people like the idea of early retirement. If you include that segment of the population who wants to retire to "a part-time job" or just "a job with time freedom," the number becomes even larger.

Most advantages to early retirement are obvious. You're younger — young enough to enjoy things you couldn't do in later retirement. Running, hiking, kayaking, and kickboxing are activities generally reserved for the young retiree. Completing an advanced degree and foreign travel also favor the younger retiree. Soon after my mother and father retired, we decided that we should go on a family trip every year or two. Our first trip was a Caribbean cruise. We had a great time and relived it often when I went to visit them in their later retirement years. Unfortunately, it was the last major trip they were able to take. A year later, their health conditions limited their travel. Still, when the family divided up my parents' estate it became apparent that, financially, they could have retired at least ten years earlier than they did! They could have had a much longer, happier retirement but chose not to because in those days "it wasn't the thing to do." Early retirement for you may include vigorous physical activities, mind stretching educational programs, exciting destinations of travel, leisure living in a resort area, and the attainment of many yet-unfulfilled life goals.

Another advantage of early retirement is a second career opportunity. In our focus groups, it became obvious that someone who enjoys their job very much might still have the desire to start a different career. Early retirement provides that opportunity. And, for some people, it will even provide the opportunity to be far more successful in their retirement years than in pre-retirement years! We've all heard the stories of everyone from artists to chicken restaurateurs who made their fortunes later in life. And even if we don't become that successful, it's the fun of trying that many times creates the happiness. These second careers often involve volunteer or semi-volunteer work. Public speaking, consulting, foster parenting, and the like are all easier to do for those who retire at earlier ages.

Early retirement also allows you to pursue your goals and experience the results while still early enough in retirement to change course if necessary. Churches are full of couples who were sure they were called to be missionaries in some foreign land. Early retirement gave them the opportunity, but it wasn't long before they figured out they were not cut out for that type of work. Their early retirement allowed them to correct their course and find their niche serving in the local area. Most of us will have the opportunity to retire only once in our lifetime. Early retirement allows for plan adjustments and course corrections.

DISADVANTAGES OF EARLY RETIREMENT

Are there any disadvantages to early retirement? Yes, there are — and they may be more substantial than you may imagine.

Insurance

First of all, if you are insured through your company, you may lose your insurance. When you walk away from the long commutes and rigid work hours, you're probably also going to say goodbye to your group health insurance. And even if you're allowed to keep it, it will cost you. In 1999, 42% of eligible retirees paid their total premium. In 1997, the figure was only 31%. If you're going to retire early, you'd better budget heavily for health insurance. It will cost you as much as $50,000 for medical coverage between ages 55 and 65. We'll talk more about health insurance in Chapter 15.

Self-Esteem

When you stop working, you may lose more than just your employer-sponsored insurance. You may feel a certain loss in self-esteem — especially if you were in an executive role or had authority over a significant group of employees. Many retired executives have trouble winding down. When they first retire, they pack their days with activities, but soon discover that being busy isn't as satisfying as being productive. Recently, I talked to a doctor who didn't want to sell *all* of his practice, because he felt he would lose his "place to hang out." That's right — he had spent so much time in the office that it had actually become a refuge for him. Retaining ownership of a small part of the practice preserved his refuge.

Friends

Another disadvantage of early retirement is that you may have no one to play with! When you were a kid, the break from school was great. The summer vacation was filled with excitement. But then one day during the school year, for some reason (which we won't go into), you found yourself home from school when the others were still attending. It was not quite as much fun, was it? You had no one to play with. Many early retirees find that the same thing is true in early retirement. You retired at age 52, but all of your friends went back to work that next Monday. You'd like to take a long weekend trip with a few of your friends, but they all have to work on Friday and be back on Monday. And even if you can occasionally do things with other people your age but who are still working, you may find that they are unwilling or unable to enjoy the lifestyle that you now have because of the wealth you have accumulated. If not properly orchestrated, early retirement may seem somewhat lonely. And, there's no lonelier sound than the lonely cry of the top dog.

Inflation

Inflation will also have a great impact on your retirement. In fact, the younger you retire, the greater effect inflation will have. As stated earlier, it is not unreasonable to expect to live as long as 30 years in retirement. After I completed my bachelor's degree, I taught high school science for three years before going on for my chiropractic degree. That was thirty years ago. Our family's total annual income was $14,000 and we were actually able to live quite well. Today, a family wage of $14,000 is a mockery. We can thank inflation for that. Although there are ups and downs, inflation historically runs three to four percent annually. Thirty years ago, a 55-year-old retiree could have lived well on $14,000 annually. Today, he would be 85 years old and struggling financially. As a result, early retirees must consider inflation even more carefully than those who retire later in life. In fact, you may find that if you retired today, the interest from your investments would provide you with only enough to live in the lifestyle you're accustomed to in "today's dollars." You may not be financially ready for retirement, especially if you do not plan to invade your principal.

In figure 3.1, you can see the affect of 3% inflation over time. Here, a retiree has $100,000 in his retirement account and receives a 7% return on that account. He needs $7,000 a year, in today's money, for living expenses. As you can see, if he lives longer than 23 years in retire-

FIG. 3.1

YEAR	BEGINNING PRINCIPAL	LIVING EXPENSES @ 3%	INTEREST @ 7%	WITHDRAWAL FROM PRINCIPAL	ENDING PRINCIPAL
1	$100,000	$7,000	$7,000	$0	$100,000
2	100,000	7,210	7,000	-210	99,790
3	99,790	7,426	6,985	-441	99,349
4	99,349	7,649	6,954	-695	98,654
5	98,654	7,879	6,906	-973	97,681
6	97,681	8,115	6,838	-1,277	96,404
7	96,404	8,358	6,748	-1,610	94,794
8	94,794	8,609	6,636	-1,973	92,821
9	92,821	8,867	6,497	-2,370	90,451
10	90,451	9,133	6,332	-2,861	87,650
11	87,650	9,407	6,136	-3,271	84,379
12	84,379	9,690	5,907	-3,783	80,596
13	80,596	9,980	5,642	-4,338	76,258
14	76,258	10,280	5,338	-4,942	71,316
15	71,316	10,588	4,992	-5,596	65,720
16	65,720	10,906	4,600	-6,306	59,414
17	59,414	11,233	4,159	-7,074	52,340
18	52,340	11,570	3,664	-7,906	44,434
19	44,434	11,917	3,110	-8,807	35,627
20	35,627	12,275	2,494	-9,781	25,846
21	25,846	12,643	1,809	-10,834	15,012
22	15,012	13,022	1,051	-11,970	3,041

ment and maintains his same standard of living (adjusted for inflation), he will use up his entire retirement savings. Had this person retired at age 55, he would be destitute by age 78. The conservative investor who plans on living entirely off investment interest will need to reinvest a portion of that interest each year as a hedge against inflation.

Being Prepared Either Way

Whether you decide to retire before age 65 or after age 65, it's good to set up milestones to gauge progress. Taking stock of your financial retirement progress provides for your security today and allows you to make corrections for security tomorrow.

20-30 YEARS BEFORE RETIREMENT

Start Saving and Investing Immediately

It's never too early to start saving for retirement. Some financial consultants suggest that until you get 15 years from retirement you will probably be spending most of your money paying off student loans, paying off business loans, buying a home, raising children, and paying for their college. They suggest that saving for retirement has a low priority if you are still 20 to 30 years from retirement. I strongly disagree! Benjamin Franklin said the most powerful force in the universe is compound interest. And, in the context of retirement, he's right! Normal wage earners who set aside 10% of their income throughout their working lives and who receive a normal rate of return on their investments are nearly guaranteed to retire as millionaires. The longer you wait to start the saving habit, the more difficult it becomes. As your income grows, your lifestyle grows. Soon you find that you're spending every dollar you make. In 1980, Americans were saving 7% of their annual incomes. In 1990, it was down to 4%. Today, the average family is saving only one-half of one percent (.5%) of their income.

Take Advantage of Tax-Deferred Savings Plans

If you have no tax-deferred savings plan at this time, you may want to consider an IRA. If your company provides a tax-deferred savings plan, enroll immediately. Many companies now match, to some extent, savings for their employees. This is as close as you can get to a windfall profit!

Insure Yourself

If you are one of the major wage earners in your family, you are probably their greatest financial asset. Insure that asset. Most types of insurance were originated to cover catastrophic events. Your premature death or disability would be a catastrophic event that could decimate the financial security of a young family. Paying insurance premiums is never fun, but it is important.

Draw Up a Will

Wills, a necessary component of good financial planning, are usually not too costly. They provide peace of mind for both the wage earners and their dependents. Though the Will may be modified many times throughout your life, it's important to have a Will early in your asset accumulation lifetime.

TEN YEARS BEFORE RETIREMENT

Study Retirement Guides

No one is as interested in your retirement success as you are. For this reason you must become the expert. Use this book as a primer — a springboard to the many other well-written retirement guides. Reading just one book on retirement a year will keep the process current in your mind and enable you to avoid the distractions and lures of indiscriminate saving and spending. On the other hand, be careful of the type of retirement guides you select. The so-called retirement guides of late-night real estate infomercial hosts and multi-level marketing companies will not work for everyone. If they worked as well as we are sometimes led to believe, every foot of shoreline from Naples to Clearwater would be lined with huge mansions — each with a Rolls Royce in the garage and a personal helicopter on the pad in the backyard...courtesy of the profits made from government foreclosure properties.

Check Out Your Company's Pension Plan or Your Own Tax-Deferred Savings Plan

How is it accumulating? How much can you expect at retirement? How will the payment be made? You are only ten years away from retirement now — it's time to start plugging in some basic numbers.

Determine Your Social Security Benefits

The Social Security Administration can provide you an estimate of what your Social Security benefits will be upon retirement. Stop by your local Social Security office or call (800) 937-2000 and ask for a Social Security Statement, previously called PEBS (Personal Earnings and Benefits Estimate Statement) form. After you have filled out and sent in the form, you will receive a report telling you of your earnings history, including how much you've contributed to Social Security. Most importantly it will indicate what benefits you can expect to receive upon reaching age 65. This report is important for two reasons: First you will have the opportunity to locate and correct any errors before retirement, and second, it will give you an idea of what impact your Social Security benefits will have on your total retirement income picture.

Concentrate on Debt Retirement

Ideally you will enter into retirement with no long-term debts. Place all these debts on a payment schedule. This means your home, vacation home, business loans, commercial real estate loans, and any other long-term debt will be paid off before or at retirement. Ten years before you retire is an excellent time to start making small additional principal payments on loans to ensure their timely payoff. You'll be surprised how little extra it takes to retire a long-term debt, such as your home loan, a few years early.

FIVE YEARS BEFORE RETIREMENT

Create a Plan to Sell Your Business

If you're self-employed, this is the time to start planning to sell your business. Maximizing the sale of your business can significantly add to your retirement nest egg.

Start Rolling Over Your Investments

When you were younger, you probably approached investing more aggressively. The liquidity of an investment was not too important when you didn't plan on needing the money for many years. You also tended to invest in investment vehicles that were designed for appreciation as opposed to "spinning off cash."

As you move toward retirement, you will want to roll a certain amount of your investments into income-producing investments, since you can only live on investment *income* and not investment *appreciation*.

Long-Term Care

Experts vary on the amount, but most agree that if you have either a very small estate (under $100,000 in value) or a very large estate (over $1 million), you may not need long-term care insurance. If the value of your estate falls within that range, you may want to consider buying long-term care (LTC) insurance. People with estates valued at less than $100,000 may not be able to afford the LTC premiums, and people with estates worth over $1 million may not need the LTC insurance in that they will be able to afford long-term care without insurance.

Look For Your Retirement Spot

Some people want to retire right where they are. Others dream of retirement communities, resort areas, or secluded bungalows. Five years before retirement is the time to start looking for that perfect spot. Buy the guides, search the maps, and travel the countryside. This is where the fun of planning for retirement begins!

Spend Time Envisioning Retirement

What will your hobbies be? Should you start them now? Will you travel? How about a degree — or another degree? Or maybe it's a second career that you've always wanted. One of the biggest mistakes a retiring person can make is to retire into nothingness.

Get Your Family's Input

Remember, your spouse is retiring, too. Do you share the same goals and ideas? Each of you may need to bend a little bit to accommodate the final plan. Your children need to know the plan, too. Regardless of their ages, you will find that they place some of their security in your stability. As your life changes, their security changes. Make them a part of the discussion.

ONE TO TWO YEARS BEFORE RETIREMENT

Determine The Date Of Your Retirement

Research your situation carefully to correctly calculate the exact date of your retirement. Be aware that retiring even as little as a month or two early can affect certain pension plans and retirement payments.

Drop Your Disability Insurance

Within your final year or two of working, you are close enough to retirement that your disability insurance will provide very little benefit. Consider dropping your disability insurance at this time.

Finalize Your Plans for the Sale of Your Business

If you own your own business, the timing of the sale of that business can be important in determining your actual date of retirement. In some cases you will want to sell your business prior to retirement and work in the business as an employee in the last few months or years.

Analyze Your Tax Obligations

Selling a business can trigger significant taxes, as can selling real estate or cashing in on tax-deferred savings plans. A few hours of planning with your accountant and financial planner may be the best time and money ever spent.

Start Planning That Second Career

As we move through the 21st Century, many retirees will find rewarding second careers. Regardless of whether you plan on being a fill-in doctor, business consultant, or entrepreneur at large, now is the time to start planning the launch of your second career. Even if you just want to retire to an unrelated part-time job, you may want to "extend your feelers" at this time.

THREE TO SIX MONTHS BEFORE RETIREMENT

Update Your Will

By this time, you have a much better idea of the value of your estate. Make any changes that are necessary to reflect your wishes.

Drop Some Insurance and Add Others

It's hard to believe, but in many cases it's a good idea to drop some of your life insurance coverage. If your retirement savings are large enough, you may not need life insurance. If you have term insurance, the premium will likely continue to rise and you may become uninsurable in the near future. If you cash in your ordinary life insurance, you can stick that money into your retirement account. But before you cash it all in, remember, there may be significant tax consequences. Most financial planners encourage you to keep a life insurance policy in place that is sufficient to pay the costs of estate taxes and legal expenses upon your death.

Along with Medicare coverage, you will want a good MediGap insurance package. MediGap insurance consists of a core group of benefits and other add-ons. Since MediGap policies vary so widely in their coverage, you will want to start early in selecting a plan to meet your needs.

Notify Your Pension Administrator of Your Retirement

Let your pension administrator know in writing at least six months ahead of time that you will be retiring. This will give them time to complete all the paper work and help you maximize your retirement benefits.

Sign Up for Social Security Benefits and Medicare Benefits

At least three months before your retirement date, notify Social Security and Medicare of your intent to retire. Fill out the proper forms to start receiving Social Security payments and Medicare coverage.

As we said earlier, most people like the idea of early retirement. And, if you plan correctly, it's very likely you can enjoy the benefits of a long, healthy, prosperous retirement. *Carpe Diem!*

4

HOW MUCH MONEY DO I NEED?

About a year ago, I was on a small ridge in the middle of a cornfield hunting Indian artifacts with Paul, a good friend and client. Our common interest in Indian history has given us some great times together. As we slowly walked the rows with the prodding sticks we used to unearth treasures, the conversation turned to retirement. Paul is just three years older than I am. He shares his expertise on Indian artifacts with me and was looking for some return information on retirement.

He explained that he was virtually debt-free and had over five million dollars in secure investments, including individual stocks, bonds, and mutual funds. In addition he had a few million more in high quality real estate, and another million in the value of his practice. When we got through running through the calculations in our heads, it appeared he was worth eight to ten million dollars. He and his wife are empty nesters and live a relatively quiet life in a small town in the southern part of the United States. Here was his question — do you think I can afford to retire? The question was so rhetorical that at first I thought he was pulling my leg just to get a reaction. Wow! I don't think it takes a Ph.D. in retirement to answer that question! If you were in your late fifties, living a modest lifestyle in a rural southern area, could you exist on eight to ten million? The answer is obvious. Sure he could retire — anytime he wanted to! How could he not draw that conclusion?

Later that night I was invited to his house for the evening meal. During the meal he told his wife, in an excited and somewhat animated way, that we had *discussed their retirement, and that I felt they could retire without financial difficulties. She was as excited as he was! Who'd have guessed it?*

WHEN IS ENOUGH, ENOUGH?

Am I saving enough? This is the most frequently asked, and perhaps the most difficult of all retirement questions. Henny Youngman once claimed he had all the money he needed — if he died by 4 o'clock that day. That's a great comedy routine, but a horrible real life experience. It can become a reality — especially in a society where life expectancy continues to elongate.

During the summer of one of my high school years I had the unique opportunity to travel around the Midwest for a metal recycling company. In the 1950s the United States had built several underground missile bases in the Midwest, and by the early '60s they were already obsolete. They were being dismantled by recycling companies for their metal contents, engines, storage tanks, and other salvageable items. As a sixteen-year-old I was quite impressed with the whole project including the missile silo, which was built thirteen stories into the Earth. As I peered over the edge during our indoctrination tour, the foreman said, "Don't worry about the fall, it won't hurt you." In surprise, I immediately questioned, "It won't?" To which he responded, "No, but the sudden stop at the bottom is a real killer." Some people enter retirement feeling they are "set for life," that they'll never need more than Social Security and their pension plan. What many don't realize is they are in a free fall through their retirement money. While it may not hurt now, the sudden stop when the bank account reads zero is a real killer.

Not too long ago, an article was written entitled *How to Retire Comfortably on 500 Thousand Dollars.* While that sounds good to people who have $500,000 or more, I don't subscribe to the "one size fits all" theory of retirement. Five hundred thousand may be plenty for one person and not enough for the next. Coming up with the answer to "how much do I need" requires making an enormous number of assumptions: How much you'll earn in retirement, what will you be able to save in retirement, how will you spend your retirement, and what will happen to the economy — just to name a few.

The amount of retirement income you need depends on the lifestyle you wish to maintain, the size of your retirement nest egg, your return on investment, and how long you live. Figure 4.0 shows your average life expectancy based on your current age. But remember, that's your *average* life expectancy. If you're 65 or younger, you could easily outlive your life expectancy by ten or fifteen years. As we said earlier, if you're within ten to fifteen years of retirement, you will probably be safe anticipating a lifespan of 90 to 95 years.

FIG. 4.0

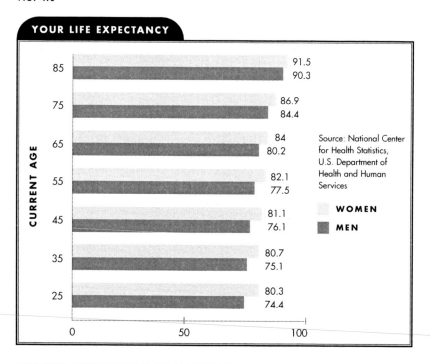

YOUR LIFE EXPECTANCY

CURRENT AGE	WOMEN	MEN
85	91.5	90.3
75	86.9	84.4
65	84	80.2
55	82.1	77.5
45	81.1	76.1
35	80.7	75.1
25	80.3	74.4

Source: National Center for Health Statistics, U.S. Department of Health and Human Services

LIVING EXPENSES IN RETIREMENT

Most retirement authorities feel the average retiree will need 70-90% of their current living expenses once they retire. We refer to it as the "80% rule." But, in this case, averages can be very misleading. Eighty percent may be a bare-bones estimate — particularly for the self-indulgent baby boomers. In our survey, unfortunately, nearly half of the respondents felt they would need less than 60% of their current income in retirement. If the authorities are right, many retirees are in for a big surprise!

Low-Income/Investment Retirees

The percentage of your current income needed in retirement is somewhat relative to your income level. Low-income retirees may need nearly as much in retirement as they did in their pre-retirement years. This is due in large part to the fact that most of their spending is for staples and very little is discretionary. They will continue to need the food, clothing, and shelter just as before.

Middle-Income/Investment Retirees

Middle-income retirees will probably see the biggest drop in cost of living during retirement years. They tend to be more financially conservative and realize they may have a limited nest egg. They are the most likely to be willing and able to downsize in retirement years.

High-Income/Investment Retirees

People who retire as multimillionaires — and there are more of them all the time — will tend to spend as much and as freely as they did in their pre-retirement years. This is true in part just because they can, and in part because many multimillionaires "slide" into retirement and have been living a somewhat semi-retired lifestyle even before retirement.

THREE STAGES OF RETIREMENT

Another reason the "80% rule" can be a dangerous assumption is that we tend to spend differently in various stages of our retirement.

The Newly Retired

Ah yes, you've retired! Now it's time to have some fun. You're

young, healthy, and full of dreams. You'll tend to fix up the house, buy
a recreational vehicle, travel to resort areas, or buy and maintain a second home. On top of that, you're used to being busy all the time and
now you have free time — time for shopping, hobbies, and social activities. You are truly living the "life of Riley." But that lifestyle comes with
a price tag. In the early years of your retirement, you can expect to spend
as much, and maybe even more, than you did in your most recent pre-
retirement years. And, since people are retiring earlier and staying
healthy longer, this "life of Riley" may continue for 15 to 20 years.

The Comfort Years

Eventually, all the hustle and bustle gives way to another type of
good life. Relaxation...quiet activities...and local events will dominate
your lifestyle. Reading a good book and watching the grandchildren will
become more important than float trips and hiking adventures. Full
winter vacations in Sun Country give way to weekend trips to friends
and family or other local events. During this period of time your spending will decrease significantly. This may account for another ten to fifteen years in retirement.

Late Retirement

As time moves on, most retirees eventually enter a time of life where
good health is their major concern. Statistics show us that half the
money we spend for health care over our entire lifetime will be spent
during the last year and a half of our life. Although Medicare, MediGap
insurance, and long-term care insurance help ease the financial burden,
health care and possibly long-term care can again cause a significant rise
in our cost of living.

Taking Advantage of Your Status

I'll have to admit that I was pretty surprised when I received my first
American Association of Retired People (AARP) solicitation for membership. After all, I had just turned fifty and didn't feel part of the

AARP generation. To make matters worse, my wife is six years younger. My first inclination was to throw it away — or hide it! But instead, I joined, and I'm glad I did. AARP provides many advantages. The discounts they have negotiated with hotels, travel groups, and product vendors are among the best and compete very favorably with AAA and other club membership discounts. Using the various senior citizen discounts makes good sense and helps preserve your retirement resources. Another advantage of most senior citizen programs is that the benefits apply equally to your spouse, even if he or she isn't of retirement age. Discounts at restaurants, movies, and educational classes can make a significant difference in your spending throughout the year.

You may also be entitled to other advantages because of your age or health condition. Senior citizens and other retirees also make up the largest segment of the handicapped population in the United States. Don't put off applying for the proper permits if you feel you are eligible. Life can become much simpler and more enjoyable if you take advantage of these benefits.

Running the Numbers

Question: How much money do I need in order to have enough for retirement?

Answer: That depends.

Don't you just hate that kind of an answer? We're conditioned to expect a specific response, but predicting your future is not an exact science and doesn't lend itself to a specific response. Changes in interest, inflation, unforeseen expenses, and additional revenue from a second job during retirement are just a few of the factors that will determine how much you have to save before retirement. The 2 + 2 of today does not necessarily equal 4 in tomorrow's dollars.

The first rule of thumb in making your money last is — do not touch your retirement accounts until you have to. The longer you continue to rack up interest the better. As a result, you should first calculate the income you will receive each month before you have to dip into your retirement account. The form in Figure 4.1 can be used as a guide. First, calculate how much money you will need for expenses each month. Then list any part-time wages you may have in retirement — royalties, Social Security, and any other regular income.   Subtract this income from the amount needed each month to meet those expenses. Your final answer will give you a good estimate of the amount of money you will have to withdraw from your retirement accounts on a monthly basis during the early years of your retirement. The example in Figure 4.2 makes the assumption that you will live on 90% of your pre-retirement income during your early retirement years.   That figure should be adjusted according to your assumptions. If you would like to be even more exact, you may want to construct an actual monthly budget and substitute that figure on line C.

The example in Figure 4.2 shows a typical scenario. This couple's pre-retirement monthly income was $6,000. After deciding which expenses would go away in retirement, they determined that they would be able to live on 90% of their pre-retirement income. This means they have an income need of $5,400 per month. Income from their part-time jobs — including wages, tips, and commissions — will be approximately $1,200 per month. They have no royalties or other similar monthly income. During their visit to their local Social Security office it was determined that they would receive approximately $1,500 per month in Social Security benefits. They also anticipate $100 per month in miscellaneous income, which brings their total income per month to $2,800. Since they will be earning $2,800 and need $5,400 to live on, they have a shortfall of $2,600. As a result, they will have to withdraw $2,600 from their retirement account each month.

BACKING INTO THE NUMBERS

If this couple needs $2,600 per month and feels they can get a 10% return on their investments, they will need a retirement nest egg of $312,000. It is computed this way: $2,600 (the amount they must with-

FIG. 4.1

MONTHLY INCOME NEEDS

A. Your Current Monthly Income ....

B. Retirement Adjustment Factor   x .90

C. Income Needed in Retirement ....

Retirement Income:

D. Wages, Tips, Commissions ....

E. Royalties ....

F. Social Security Benefits ....

G. Miscellaneous Income ....

H. Total Income (D-G) ....

I. Additional Money Needed (Line C minus Line H) ....

FIG. 4.2

MONTHLY INCOME NEEDS

A. Your Current Monthly Income $6,000

B. Retirement Adjustment Factor   x .90

C. Income Needed in Retirement $5,400

Retirement Income:

D. Wages, Tips, Commissions $1,200

E. Royalties   0

F. Social Security Benefits $1,500

G. Miscellaneous Income $ 100

H. Total Income (D-G) $2,800

I. Additional Money Needed (Line C minus Line H) $2,600 draw from retirement funds monthly) X 12 (the number of months in a year) = $31,200, or 10% return of their $312,000 investment.

Anticipating a 10% return on investment is a very aggressive assumption. If the couple anticipates a more likely return of 5%, after taxes and reinvestment for inflation, they would need a nest egg of $624,000.

HOW WILL YOU CALCULATE YOUR RETIREMENT NEEDS?

It is obvious that your needs can change when your assumptions change. Each of us must make his own assumptions and come up with his own plan. Here are the three most common:

Plan 1: Live On Both Principal and Interest
Rating: Very dangerous.

You're actually planning on spending your last dollar on the very day you die. Unpredictable factors — like increased lifespan, decreased return on investment, catastrophic illnesses, or inflation — can undermine this plan instantly.

For the first half of my career in chiropractic practice, I was a solo practitioner. Then another doctor who was a few years older than I was approached me about practicing together. He was a certified Athletic Trainer, Registered Physical Therapist, and Doctor of Chiropractic, and he wanted to avoid the business hassles involved with a practice. We agreed to terms, and he became an associate. He had a good practice and practiced actively until he reached age 42. Then, his practice started to decline rapidly. In conversation he related to me that both his mother and father had died of natural causes at age 42. He felt he may be living on borrowed time and just wanted to retire and enjoy life more. My immediate question was, "Are you financially prepared to enter retirement?" He responded that he and his wife had no children and, therefore, there was no "inheritance" factor. He said, "As far as I'm concerned I'd like to spend my last dollar the last day I'm alive." Then he demonstrated his plan by laying an imaginary dollar on the top of his desk and slumping down in his chair!

This plan is very simple. You plan on spending all of your money — principal and interest — before you die. You simply anticipate your expected lifespan and your anticipated return on investment. Then calculate how much money you can withdraw (and live on) on a monthly basis throughout your anticipated lifespan. Here's an example: A 65-year-old man anticipates that he will live to be 85 years old — another twenty years. He has $300,000 in savings and anticipates a 10% return on investment. At that rate, according to Figure 4.3, he can withdraw $34,740 per year ($2,895 per month).

FIG. 4.3

YEAR	RETIREMENT SAVINGS	INTEREST INCOME @ 10%	SPENDABLE INCOME
1	$300,000	$29,777	$34,740
2	$295,037	$29,256	$34,740
3	$289,553	$28,681	$34,740
4	$283,494	$28,047	$34,740
5	$276,801	$27,346	$34,740
6	$269,407	$26,572	$34,740
7	$261,239	$25,717	$34,740
8	$252,216	$24,772	$34,740
9	$242,248	$23,728	$34,740
10	$231,236	$22,575	$34,740
11	$219,071	$21,302	$34,740
12	$205,633	$19,894	$34,740
13	$190,787	$18,340	$34,740
14	$174,387	$16,622	$34,740
15	$156,269	$14,726	$34,740
16	$136,255	$12,630	$34,740
17	$114,145	$10,315	$34,740
18	$89,720	$7,751	$34,740
19	$62,731	$4,938	$34,740
20	$32,929	$1,811	$34,740

Again, remember, this type of planning is very dangerous. If he happens to outlive his anticipated lifespan, fails to achieve a 10% return on investment, or meets with any other catastrophes, he may live his later years destitute and dependent on the welfare system.

Plan 2: Live on Interest Only
Rating: Not bad, pretty logical, but still a little risky.

The concept sounds good — but how do you adjust for inflation in your later retirement years? Thirty years ago, the average teacher's wage was eight to ten thousand dollars. Would you be willing to live on that today? Will you be able to live on today's wage in thirty years?

On the surface, amassing enough net worth to live only on your interest sounds like the perfect plan. That way you'll never outlive your money! The problem is that inflation can quickly erode your spending power. Figure 4.4 shows the historical rate of inflation in the United States from 1945 to 1990. As you can see, there is no thirty-year span of time when we did not see periods of significant inflation. Many major institutions use 4% as their inflation adjustment rate when doing long-term planning. On the other hand, many financial planners feel like a 4% inflation rate is too high and suggest using 3% as your inflation adjustment factor. In addition, we should realize an individual's inflation rate may not necessarily match the nation's inflation rate, if that individual is not using the sectors of the economy that comprise the national inflation number. For example, if housing and gasoline prices have pushed up cost of living numbers in the United States, but you live in a home you own and do very little traveling, your personal inflation rate may be lower than the national average. I feel 3% is a logical inflation factor to use when figuring long-term inflation rates.

FIG. 4.4

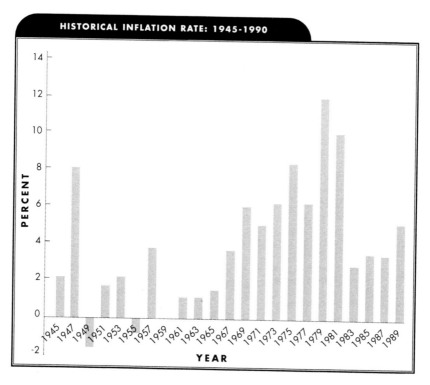

HISTORICAL INFLATION RATE: 1945-1990

There is some good news. If you calculate your retirement income based on interest only and inflation does become a factor, you do have your principal to fall back on. While most people who subscribe to the "interest only" philosophy hate to dip into their principal, it does become more permissible when we reach our later retirement years.

Plan 3: Live On Interest Only, With Any Inflation Factor
Rating: Conservative, but logical.

Of the three concepts, I like this one the best by far and use it as my personal guide to retirement. Even though it may be overly conservative, it is by far the safest.

This concept allows us to spend only a portion of our retirement income interest. The remaining portion is reinvested into the retirement account as a hedge against inflation. Taxes are also figured into this plan. For example, if you receive a 10% return on your retirement savings, you will pay taxes with the first 2% and reinvest another 3% back into the retirement account, leaving 5% to live on. This means that if your retirement account has a value of $3 million and you receive 10% interest, your total investment interest will be $300,000 per year. Of that $300,000, at least $60,000 will be paid in taxes, leaving $240,000. Another $90,000 should be reinvested into your retirement account to compensate for inflation, and you will live on the net amount of $150,000 plus any other income, such as wages and Social Security. Figure 4.5 illustrates this example.

FIG. 4.5

YEAR	RETIREMENT VALUE	INTEREST INCOME @ 10%	TAXES @ 20%	INFLATION REINVESTMENT @3%	SPENDABLE INCOME
1	$3,000,000	$300,000	$60,000	$90,000	$150,000
2	$3,090,000	$309,000	$61,800	$92,700	$154,500
3	$3,182,700	$318,270	$63,654	$95,481	$159,135
4	$3,278,181	$327,818	$65,564	$98,345	$163,909
5	$3,376,526	$337,653	$67,531	$101,296	$168,826
6	$3,477,822	$347,782	$69,556	$104,335	$173,891
7	$3,582,157	$358,216	$71,643	$107,465	$179,108
8	$3,689,622	$368,962	$73,792	$110,689	$184,481
9	$3,800,310	$380,031	$76,006	$114,009	$190,016
10	$3,914,320	$391,432	$78,286	$117,430	$195,716
11	$4,031,749	$403,175	$80,635	$120,952	$201,587
12	$4,152,702	$415,270	$83,054	$124,581	$207,635
13	$4,277,283	$427,728	$85,546	$128,318	$213,864
14	$4,405,601	$440,560	$88,112	$132,168	$220,280
15	$4,537,769	$453,777	$90,755	$136,133	$226,888
16	$4,673,902	$467,390	$93,478	$140,217	$233,695
17	$4,814,119	$481,412	$96,282	$144,424	$240,706
18	$4,958,543	$495,854	$99,171	$148,756	$247,927
19	$5,107,299	$510,730	$102,146	$153,219	$255,365
20	$5,260,518	$526,052	$105,210	$157,816	$263,026

YOUR PLAN MAKES A DIFFERENCE

It's easy to see how some people are lulled into a sense of false security. Slight miscalculations or misassumptions, as well as the plan you choose, can make a big difference. For example, if you feel you need to withdraw an additional $4,000 per month to live on in retirement, believe you can maintain a 10% ROI, and plan to live twenty years in retirement, you will need $415,640 if you use Plan A. If you use plan B you'll need $480,000, and $686,000 if you subscribe to Plan C.

If you are not sure you are saving enough for your retirement, there are plenty of online calculators that will do the math for you. But again, you will have to make a few assumptions — so make sure you are entering realistic ones — like an average 10% return on your investments rather than the 20% return they earned last year. One of the best online calculators is the **Quicken Retirement Planner** (www.quicken.com). This site has one of the most comprehensive retirement calculators in cyberspace. It gives you information on a long list of factors that affect your retirement, including personal savings, Social Security benefits and even your tax rate after retirement. Another good online calculator is the **American Savings Education Council** (www.asec.org), but the calculator assumes you will need 70% of your current income, that you will live to age 87, and that you will have a constant real rate of return of 3% after inflation.

EFFECTS OF EARLY RETIREMENT

While it's great to think about early retirement, the calculations in this chapter may have led you to the conclusion that you don't have as much money as you will need in order to retire. In that case you may think about working a year or two longer. You're not alone. Although the retirement age of Americans has dropped in the last few decades, recent studies show it may be leveling off and even reversing. Postponing your retirement and stashing the extra money away in your retirement account can produce a substantial increase in your retirement savings. If you're making $90,000 per year and contributing 10% to your

401(k), with a 5% match from your employer and a 5% return, a $500,000 portfolio would be worth $580,734 in just two more years. In fact, as good as early retirement sounds, it has some financial drawbacks.

1. You will earn less over your lifetime.
2. You may contribute less to your retirement account.
3. You will start to spend your retirement income earlier.
4. You will lose the interest on the money you spent while in early retirement.

Besides that, if you continue to work, you will to an extent avoid the effects of inflation during those last working years. And you will reduce the risk of what happens to the national economy and your return on investment in the years between early and late retirement. If your investment return is low during those first years, you may be forced to dip into your principal. Conversely, if you're working, you will be supported by your wage.

The effects of early retirement can be seen quite vividly using the Quicken Retirement Planner. After you have entered the required retirement information into the online calculator, you can change your retirement age and the calculator will automatically compute the effect on your retirement savings.

HOW MUCH DO YOU REALLY HAVE?

It is obvious (Figure 4.5) that living a more upscale lifestyle in retirement requires a fairly significant retirement account. And while that's true, you may have a larger retirement nest egg than you realize. In fact, your savings accounts may grow in retirement. Many people receive an inheritance in the early part of their retirement. Any inheritance monies directed into your retirement account adds to your security and increases the chance of creating an inheritance for your children. If you downsize homes, excess proceeds from the sale can also be added to your retirement account. And selling a business or business-related assets can add to your retirement nest egg.

Maximize the sale of those assets. For example, be sure your house is in good repair. Increase its "street appeal" with inexpensive cosmetic changes. Consider selling your house on your own to avoid realtor fees.

Our company recently worked with a doctor who was in the process of selling his practice and moving into retirement. We determined that his practice was so large that it would be best handled by two doctors, and by selling the practice to two doctors it made it easier for them to qualify for loans and he could maximize the amount of the sale.

These sometimes unanticipated injections into your retirement account, coupled with the fact that most people begin retirement relatively debt-free, can create an extra cushion. But be careful of "lifestyle creep" — slowly spending more money as you become more comfortable in retirement. At the end of each year you should analyze your financial status — including any increases in spending or decreases in income — and make any corrections to your financial retirement plan.

5

IF YOU STILL HAVE TIME TO SAVE

E veryone feels a different urgency regarding saving for retirement. About five years ago our firm was working with a client in his late 50s who had narrowly escaped bankruptcy just a few years earlier. He was still heavily laden with debt. He owed the IRS back taxes, and all his assets were totally encumbered. His financial picture was a mess! On the other hand, he was an excellent family man, had a good practice, and his patients loved him. As we looked closer, we realized that with his highly profitable practice, modest standard of living (in a rural area of the northeast) and good work ethic, he had a great opportunity to turn his financial life around before retirement. We arranged to meet him for a private consultation after one of our Philadelphia area seminars. Three of us met in a hotel suite around a conference table.

My partner had laid out a plan for him that consisted of refinancing old debts, making non-deductible loans deductible, paying off loans early, and canceling significant amounts of IRS interest and penalties. All the pieces fell into place and it became obvious that he could retire within ten years — debt-free and with $400,000 in the bank! My partner and I were excited about the plan, but in the middle of explaining it to the client, he casually got up from the table, walked across the room, opened a soft drink and asked a totally unrelated question. He had absolutely no interest in saving for retirement. He preferred to take the ostrich approach — sticking his head in the sand. The consultation ended without ever explaining the rest of the plan — and the client didn't even notice!

HOW MUCH TIME DO YOU HAVE LEFT?

Today, there are more opportunities to invest than at any time in history. Online brokerage companies are paying millions of dollars for TV spots during the Super Bowl, NBA Championships, and any other media event that draws a crowd! The average investor can buy or sell stock for as little as $8 per trade — in some cases it's even free! And the Internet makes more investment information available than ever before. Still, thousands of households — even high-income households — have somehow managed to save very little.

Nearly half of the people in America between ages 22 and 61 have saved less than $10,000 for retirement. Americans' savings over the last two decades have spiraled down from over 8% of their annual earnings in 1980 to less than 1% today. In fact, according to the AARP, only one fifth of the baby boomers have more than $25,000 in assets, and the bad news is you may be one of them!

Having read to this point, some people are feeling more comfortable with the amount of their retirement savings and others less comfortable. If you realize that you may need more retirement savings and have a few years before retirement, there are some things that you can do starting now.

PUT YOUR SAVINGS PLAN IN HIGH GEAR

If you plan on working another five to ten years, you still have a great opportunity. Saving just $500 per month at 8% interest for ten years will increase your retirement savings by $91,066 and, if you don't touch that amount, it will increase to $200,534 ten years into your retirement.

Early in your working career, saving seemed hard and had a low priority. Now, as retirement nears, saving money is becoming a necessity. Perhaps the best way to save is by having a certain amount automatically deducted from every paycheck. If your employer has a tax-deferred savings plan, consider maximizing your contribution — this is especially true if the employer has some type of matching program. If you're self-employed or your employer does not have a retirement plan, consider opening a savings account and instructing your bank to transfer money from your checking account to your savings (retirement) account at regular intervals. Many people have their auto-withdrawals coincide with their pay periods so the same amount is deducted from their checking accounts on each payday.

UNLOAD ANY UNNECESSARY DEBT

One impediment to saving is a high debt load. The more debt you carry, the more payments you must make. The more payments you make, the less opportunity you have to save. Make a list of all your recurring monthly payments. Many times you will find that you are making payments on items and services that you no longer want. A boat, a second car, business equipment you no longer use, and health club memberships usually top the list. Collision insurance on older cars can be cancelled, and some disability insurance can even be dropped if you're getting close to retirement.

SWEAR OFF NEW DEBT

In our survey of working professionals we found that 89% currently have debt, but only 7% say they will have any significant debt when they enter retirement. The amount of money you need in retirement can be reduced in direct proportion to the amount of debt you pay off before retirement. But even an aggressive debt retirement plan cannot make you debt free if new debts are continually added. And carrying high-interest debt — especially high-interest consumer debt — greatly diminishes your capacity to accelerate your savings plan. As a family, make an agreement not to take on any new debt.

SELL THE UNNEEDED

One quick way to get out of debt and improve your retirement nest egg is to sell everything you have that you no longer need. It's amazing what people come up with. Vacation homes that are no longer used; a second, third or fourth car; boats; motorcycles; business equipment; and sporting/exercise equipment usually top the list. A good, old-fashioned garage sale can get rid of clutter and generate money to pay off debt and increase savings.

UNLOAD ANY DEAD WEIGHT

Dead weight is defined as any person or thing that you are maintaining that has no real value to you. Don't misunderstand, I'm not suggesting that you sell your teenagers or divorce your spouse. Instead, I'm talking about the "free ride" that some people may be enjoying at your expense.

Sometimes it's difficult to say no to family members or friends. But the free ride has to end sometime. Adult children should be self-supporting. Continuing to provide support for adult children simply creates a generation of economic cripples. Then there are family members who continue to borrow small amounts of money over time without definite plans (or intent) to repay you. That, too, must stop if you are going to build your retirement nest egg. Sometimes these free handouts are thinly veiled as some type of compensation. Allowing your children (especially adult children) to do errands for you with pay considerably above the market rate, or having family members work in your business even though they are not as productive as non-family members, are good examples of money management procedures that can stifle your retirement savings.

Dead weight, as we define it, is not limited to people. Providing ongoing financial support of projects in which you are no longer interested or contributing to every volunteer organization that calls can have the same negative effect on your retirement savings.

CONSTRUCT A LOAN REPAYMENT PLAN

Many retirees will be able to live on 60-70% of their pre-retirement income simply because they have orchestrated their final debt repayment so it coincides with their retirement date. This is especially true if the debts are long-term debts. For example, a working couple who now needs $6,000 per month to live on may be able to live on $4,000 per month in retirement since they will be making their last home payment, college loan payment (for their children), and retirement savings contribution before they retire. Unfortunately, one of the biggest deterrents to retiring this *long-term* debt is excess *short-term* debt. Credit cards, car payments, personal loans and other consumer debt items are generally financed at a relatively high-interest rate and are not tax deductible. As a result, they devour a large portion of each paycheck making long-term debt reduction and retirement savings difficult and a low priority.

Retiring debt-free has a nice ring to it. And with the exception of such things as extremely low interest loans and loans with repayment penalties, you will want to enter retirement debt-free. Constructing a loan repayment plan and following the plan is easier than you may imagine. Start by shifting all your high-interest debts, such as credit cards, to low interest, tax deductible loans like a home equity loan. One couple who had $16,000 in credit card debts with an average interest rate of 16.75% consolidated those debts with an 8.75% home equity loan. Because the home equity loan was tax deductible, it had the net effect of a 6.75% interest rate — the couple saved 10%.

Create a chart like shown in Figure 5.1. Include the amount remaining on each debt, the interest rate, and the monthly payment. Then decide which debts should be paid first based on interest rate. As a rule of thumb, you will want to pay off your highest interest debts first. Before you assign each debt an order of pay off, make sure that you take into account any debts where the interest is tax deductible. For instance, your home loan interest is deductible and while the value of that deduction varies according to your income tax bracket, you can generally assume that it has the effect of lowering the interest rate by two percentage points. In other words, if your home loan (or home equity loan) is at 8.5%, and you have a personal loan (which is not deductible) at 7.5%, you would be better off financially by paying the 7.5% loan off first. Since your house loan at 8.5% is tax deductible, it has the after-tax equivalent of 6.5%.

Once you have completed your debt repayment chart and have determined the order of pay off, start your repayment plan by making double payments on the first (highest interest) loan. Notify the lender that all additional monies should be applied to principal only. Ask them to respond in writing acknowledging your request. Since the additional payment will apply totally to principal, your highest interest loan should be paid off very rapidly.

Once the first loan is paid off, attack the second loan by paying your regular payment plus all additional monies now available because the first loan has been paid off. Continue this process of applying all additional monies to each successive loan. Figure 5.2 demonstrates this repayment procedure.

FIG. 5.1

LOAN	BALANCE	INTEREST RATE	PAYMENT
VISA (5513)	$1,381.00	17%	$225.00
MC (4716)	$634.00	18%	$106.00
HOUSE	$62,000	8.5%	$695.00
CAR	$1,850.00	11%	$460.00
FATHER	$6,000.00	6%	$0.00
COLLEGE LOAN	$8,000.00	12%	$205.00
SEARS	$654.00	17%	$138.00
HOME EQUITY	$9,000.00	9%	$300.00
TAXES	$1,200.00	12%	$160.00
ALIMONY	$24,000.00	0%	$1,000.00

APPLY EXTRA MONEY TO YOUR WEALTH ACCOUNT

Once you have paid off your debts — or at least your high-interest debt — you will find you have much more spendable income. Perhaps "spendable" income is a misnomer. That income now must go into your retirement account.

We encourage our clients to place any unexpected income in the wealth account, too. Refunds, loan paybacks, returned deposits, dividends, and inheritance should all be deposited into your wealth account immediately. Making an immediate deposit serves two purposes. First,

you start earning interest immediately and, second, you avoid the temp-
tation to spend it.

If you didn't start your retirement savings as early as you should
have, you must play catch up. That includes retiring debt quickly, saving aggressively, and getting a good return on investment.

FIG. 5.2   LOAN REPAYMENT PLAN

LOAN	BALANCE	INTEREST RATE	PAYMENT	PAYOFF ORDER	MONTHS*
VISA (5513)	$1,381.00	17%	$225.00	#3	3 months
			$350.00		
			$575.00		
MC (4716)	$634.00	18%	$106.00	#1	3 months
			$106.00		
			$212.00		
HOUSE	$62,000	8.5% (6.5%)	$695.00		
CAR	$1,850.00	11%	$460.00	#6	0 months
			$940.00		
			$1,400.00		
FATHER	$6,000.00	6%			
COLLEGE LOAN	$8,000.00	12%	$205.00	#5	10 months
			$735.00		
			$940.00		
SEARS	$654.00	17%	$135.00	#2	2 months
			$212.00		
			$350.00		
HOME EQUITY	$9,000.00	9% (7%)	$300.00		
TAXES	$1,200.00	12%	$160.00	#4	2 months
			$575.00		
			$735.00		
ALIMONY	$24,000.00	0%	$1,000.00		

*Months needed to retire debt after double payments start.

6
TYPES
OF RETIREMENT

Look at the letter I received yesterday.

Hello Dave:

I would appreciate your input on a topic I am beginning to accumulate information on — the potential sale of my practice.

In the early 90s, I developed a game plan for early retirement by 2012. I selected this year because that's when the youngest of our four children will graduate high school and I will be 55. My retirement goal has been to accumulate $6 million by 2012. Well, it seems I am slightly ahead of schedule. If my returns continue at their current rate, I will likely have the $6 million accumulated in my IRA by 2003. So, I have begun to think about retiring ahead of schedule and devoting the balance of my life to charity and missionary work.

As you know, under current tax law, the Internal Revenue Service allows for early retirement without the 10% penalty tax if you take "substantially equal periodic payments." The IRS provides guidelines to allow one to do this.

In preparation for possibly making a mid-life change after 20 years of practice, I am writing to inquire if you know of any formula(s) that you or other doctors have used to establish the fair market value of their practice. I recognize there are many ways to establish the value for a practice, and the bottom line is, "what the buyer and seller can agree upon", but I would like to begin getting familiar with what others have done.

This possible life change is nothing I am going to do without a lot of discernment and prayer, but am just trying to get my "ducks in a row" should the retirement money be available at an earlier date than I previously planned and I decide to move into retirement.

Thanks for your help. I look forward to hearing from you and seeing you in Minneapolis in the near future.

Frank Collins

Most people would love to have Frank's dilemma — at age 46 he'll have $6 million in his retirement account! Actually, he has lots of options, but do you know what caught my eye? The fact that he knew what he wanted to do in retirement. Remember, he's only 43-years old.

HOW WILL YOU MOVE INTO RETIREMENT?

How will you move into retirement? Will you just quit one day at 5 o'clock and not come back, or will you "slide" into retirement? Fifty percent of people who are five to ten years away from retirement say they will still work in some capacity once they reach retirement. In our most recent survey of working health care professionals, 66% said they planned to work at least part-time in retirement. Some will stay with their current occupations, others will try their hand at something new. Visit a job fair today and you'll see as many people over fifty-five years old as under. Other new retirees are taking classes, becoming certified or receiving company training, which will allow them to work as sales people, realtors or in a host of other occupations. In the early days of Social Security, retirement almost always meant, "doing nothing." This was in part due to the fact that life expectancy in retirement was less than five years. Today it more likely signals the beginning of the next third of your life. We can now work a little and still play. In fact, now that we're retired, our work can be our play!

FULL RETIREMENT VS. PARTIAL RETIREMENT

Full retirement or partial retirement — the choice is yours. Neither is wrong and both have advantages. If retirement for you means spending the rest of your days sailing the South Pacific — go for it! Thirty percent of our clients plan to move directly into full-time retirement. On the other hand, if you like the prestige, self-esteem, challenges, and relationships that working provides, then phased-in retirement may be your cup of tea. Continuing to work part-time does have its advantages. Continued company insurance, business deductions, travel opportunities and a place to just hang out are sometimes reason enough to keep the retirement-aged person working. Working part-time in your early years of retirement can also work magic with your retirement savings. It not only allows you to take less out of your retirement savings, it also provides time for your savings to accumulate.

RETIREMENT OPTIONS

There are about as many retirement options as there are retirees — and business owners have even more options available.

Full Retirement

Full retirement — America's dream. And, the right decision for many. It provides opportunity to move to a new location, concentrate on hobbies and just flat enjoy life!

Partial Retirement — Part-time

Some people just love their work! I recently received notice that the oldest practicing chiropractor in our state entered total retirement. He is 94 years old. For him, retirement began twenty years ago by simply working less. Over the years, he continued to reduce his schedule until finally he was working just a half-day per week. If you love your profession and see your work as your mission, it's a great way to retire.

Partial Retirement — Tandem Practice

Some professionals move into retirement by working in tandem with a partner or partners that take over a portion of the workload. Ten years ago, my asset protection attorney handled all aspects of my asset protection needs. Today, his two sons, an attorney and financial planner, work in tandem with their father to provide those services. I simply talk to "the next one available." It works well and allows me to slowly transfer to someone in the firm who is younger than I am and will be available throughout my entire retirement. One dental office has three generations of dentists working. While each maintains his own patient base, patients from the eldest dentist can easily be seen by the other two as the older dentist continues to move into retirement. Two Daytona Beach realtors work together as a team. They sell a lot of real estate. They are both over seventy.

Partial Retirement — Management

Business owners who are tired of performing the day-to-day functions of the business may enjoy retiring into a management capacity in the business. This management may be time sensitive — which means the day-to-day functions must be done during business hours — or non-time sensitive — which allows for management at the retiree's discretion. Management that is not time sensitive allows for much more freedom in retirement.

Retire Into Paraprofessional Activities

When a person retires, especially a professional, years of education, training and experience are lost. A professional may prefer to pass this information on by working part-time in the profession as a consultant, teacher, speaker or author.

Retire Into A New Career

Some professions do not lend themselves well for transition to part-time work, and some retirees just prefer a professional change of scenery. One elementary school principal retired into a new profession. He now sells prepaid legal services. Though he loved his work, he enjoys the change of pace and the additional income. To give yourself the best chance of success, pick a business that matches the retirement lifestyle you have chosen. If you want time freedom in retirement, choose a retirement career that lets you work the hours you want to work. If you hate long commutes, find a retirement career that allows you to work from home.

Retire Into Your Calling

Some people have worked all their life in a job. It wasn't their true calling and they knew it, but the risk of restarting a career in mid-life was too great. Now, in retirement, they can pursue their calling — their first love. Motivational books are full of stories of people who found their calling and great success in their retirement years.

Just Take Any Old Job

It sounds unexciting, but sometimes it's a good idea. It gets us out of the house, it keeps us in society, and it gives us something to do. It's low stress and it gives us a little income.

Seasonal Retirement

Here's a great idea. Retire ten months out of the year and work two! One doctor, now retired, works 40-60 hours per week in August and September making designer candles.

Early in October, he delivers his candles to boutiques for holiday sales. He makes great money. Another retiree works as temporary Christmas help at the department store she retired from.

Working for a few months has its advantages. First, you make money to live on during the working cycle, and second, you stop spending retirement savings a few months each year. It also keeps you in circulation — something that becomes important as you age.

Work 'Til You Die

It's true! Some people's goal is not to retire and that's fine, too. In our latest retirement survey, 3.9% of the respondents said they plan on never retiring. One of my first patients was the daughter of an osteopath who always said he wanted to practice until he died. One day, this 84-year-old doctor had just finished working on the last patient scheduled that day when he said, "I think that's all I'm going to be able to do." He walked into his private office, sat down in his chair, laid his head on his desk, and passed away. To each his own!

IF YOU CAN'T RETIRE

Some retirement-age people reach retirement with virtually no savings and no retirement plan. Although their options become severely limited, there are still steps to take, which can provide a certain degree of security for later life.

Switch Jobs

If your lifestyle, debt load, or lack of retirement savings will force you to work during retirement, you may want to consider moving to a less challenging job that you will be able to perform into your retirement years. You may also want to find a job that will allow you to move from full-time to part-time as you get older.

Conserve Finances

Review your budget; there may be significant savings available. For instance, there is no rule that says you must pay for your children's college educations. You could instead give them a low-interest loan, which can be repaid to you in your retirement years.

Social Security Disability

If you have an impairment that prevents you from working, you may be eligible for Social Security disability. I worked with one middle-aged man who had frequent seizures of unknown origin. It precluded him from most meaningful employment. Even a job as a short-order cook was a risk, in that during a seizure he could fall forward onto the grill! We worked to get his seizures classified as a form of epilepsy, which then made him eligible for Social Security disability. It is often difficult to qualify for Social Security disability because of the Social Security Administration's strict definition of disability, but if you have true disability, you should apply now for assistance.

Offspring Help

Children…for thirty years you washed them, dressed them and fed them. Perhaps now they can help you in return. As you enter retirement consider moving to an area that will allow your children to assist you.

Voluntary Organizations

Churches and other volunteer groups are known for their willingness to help those in need. And while your purpose in joining a church is not for "free help," being active in a church may have that effect.

Reverse Mortgage

If you're fortunate enough to own your own home, you may consider a reverse mortgage. With a reverse mortgage, a bank will provide you monthly payments which build as debt against your home. When your estate is settled the bank will receive proceeds from the home as needed to satisfy the reverse mortgage.

As you can imagine, life in retirement without a nest egg severely limits your retirement options. But if you're not yet at retirement age, don't consign yourself to a mediocre retirement lifestyle quite yet. All baby boomers have heard stories about the Great Depression from their parents. Most boomers treat it in a "yeah, yeah, yeah, I'm sick of hearing about this" mentality, but for your parents and grandparents it was real! Many people lost everything they had. My grandfather, with a family of nine children, was one of them. Yet, even after mid-life financial devastation he was able to reacquire assets, which allowed him to live in retirement to 93 years old (and his wife to 96). He was also able to provide an inheritance to each of his six living children of over $20,000 — equal to two to three year's wages at that time.   As Yogi Berra so profoundly put it, "It ain't over 'til it's over."

7

WHAT ABOUT SOCIAL SECURITY?

I t seems today that everyone is complaining about Social Security. Complaints include bureaucratic red tape, inadequacy and even insolvency. I'm reminded of times when, as a child, I would complain. My mother would recite the phrase, "I complained because I had no shoes until I met a man without any feet." In 1935, as part of the New Deal, the Federal government created the Social Security system so American workers would have an income after they were no longer able to work. When Social Security began paying retirement benefits, the American male who reached adulthood, had a life expectancy of about sixty-three years. If a man did live until age sixty-five, he had a life expectancy of another two to three years. At that same time, most women did not work outside the home. When their husbands died, they were frequently left without a means of income. As a result, Social Security set a policy allowing surviving spouses with dependent children under sixteen and spouses over sixty to collect benefits based on what their working spouse had contributed to the Social Security system. Some consider Social Security as the greatest anti-poverty program in the history of mankind. Today, less than 10% of our elderly live in poverty — lower than the rate for working age Americans.

Before Social Security 50% of the elderly lived in poverty. My grandmother was one of them. She was born in the late 1800s to a poor farm family and with a birth defect — a fairly severe hare lip and cleft palate. Surgical procedures of the day improved function but did very little to improve general appearance. At age seventeen she married a man whose previous wife had died *in childbirth. She immediately became the stepmother of two small boys. Together, she and her husband had four additional children. Her husband, too, was a farmer, but died at an early age and without retirement savings. For her, even the small amount of retirement benefits she received was a blessing! Perhaps Social Security isn't as bad as it is made out to be.*

WILL SOCIAL SECURITY BE AROUND?

As with Mark Twain, the rumors of Social Security's death have been greatly exaggerated. There are some people who believe that the Social Security system, as it is today, is going to collapse of its own weight just when baby boomers reach retirement age. They cite many reasons including the swelling crop of baby boomers (seventy-six million) that will move from paying taxes to receiving benefits over the next few decades. But recently the Social Security Administration reported that the retirement fund has gained another three years of solvency and won't come up short until the year 2037, and even after 2037 they will still be able to meet 72% of the budget. Couple that with the recent national debt turn-around and we may likely have solvency for the next fifty years.

EARNINGS PENALTY LIFTED

Here's more good news! Recently the earnings limit for Social Security recipients ages 65 and older who continue to work has been eliminated. In the past, we lost one dollar for every three dollars earned above $17,000 per year. This meant that we were paying an additional 33% tax on our earnings. As of January 1, 2000, that penalty was eliminated.

The penalty was originally imposed to encourage older workers to leave the job market and make room for younger workers. Now, with the unemployment rate at a historic low, that's no longer a concern. Critics also felt the penalty was unfair because it applied only to earned income, hurting those people who needed to continue to work in retirement. It did not apply to investment income, savings interest, dividends or capital gains.

So once again, Social Security seems alive and well.

SHOULD I COLLECT AT SIXTY-TWO?

Before you "run the numbers" to determine when you should retire, you should consider the non-financial factors.

Health

If you're in good health and it appears you'll have a long life span, you may want to continue working. On the other hand, if your health is becoming a factor in your quality of life during your last years of working, you may decide sixty-two is the right age.

Aspirations

Early retirement may allow you to work on your yet-unrealized dreams. I recently talked with a 60-year-old auto mechanic who worked on the fleet of cars owned by the local university. Earlier in his life, he traveled professionally as a public speaker and was quite successful. But married life and family obligations pulled him off the road. While he enjoys his present occupation, his heart is that of a public speaker. He has maintained a small schedule of speaking engagements and is confident that he could return to public speaking as a part-time job. For this empty nester, the call of the stage may make sixty-two a perfect retirement age.

Your Spouse

The age of your spouse and his or her interests in retirement must also be considered. Many times an older partner will continue to work until age sixty-five if his or her partner is significantly younger, enjoys working, and is in good health.

Stress of the Job

Some jobs are naturally more stressful — and more physically

demanding — than other jobs. During private practice as a chiropractor, I found that certain occupations predisposed their workers to an
early retirement. Bricklayers and cement workers almost always showed
the effects of their labor in their lower lumbar spine. If your job is high
stress — physically or psychologically — you may opt for early retirement.

WHEN CAN I RETIRE WITH FULL BENEFITS?

Today, if you retire at age sixty-two, you will receive 70-80% of the
amount that you would receive if you were to retire at age sixty-five.
The way Social Security is structured, you will become eligible to receive
your full benefits sometime between the age of sixty-five and sixty-seven,
depending on your year of birth. The chart in figure 7.1 will help you
determine your "full benefits" retirement date.

In our survey of executives, a vast majority (92%) expected Social
Security to provide less than 30% of income needed in retirement —
and they're probably right! Even for the average wage earner, Social
Security will replace only 40% of their previous income.

FIG. 7.1

IF YOU WERE BORN IN...	YOU CAN'T COLLECT YOUR FULL BENEFIT UNTIL AGE...	HOW MUCH YOU LOSE IF YOU START COLLECTING AT AGE 62
1937 & earlier	65	20.00%
1938	65 & 2 months	20.83%
1939	65 & 4 months	21.67%
1940	65 & 6 months	22.50%
1941	65 & 8 months	23.33%
1942	65 & 10 months	24.17%
1943-1954	66	25.00%
1955	66 & 2 months	25.84%
1956	66 & 4 months	26.66%
1957	66 & 6 months	27.50%
1958	66 & 8 months	28.33%
1959	66 & 10 months	29.17%
1960 & later	67	30.00%

HOW MUCH WILL I GET?

The amount of your Social Security benefits depends on the amount of time you've worked and how much you have paid in. In 2001, the top benefit for a single retiree was about $1,536 per month, up from $1,433 in year 2000. By the same token, the average monthly benefit today is $907 per month for a man and $699 per month for a woman. For an exact determination, you should visit your local Social Security office. And as mentioned earlier, you may want to contact Social Security now and request a Social Security Statement, previously called a Personal Earnings and Benefits Estimate Statement (PEBS) form. You can get this form from your local Social Security office or by calling 800-234-5772. The Social Security web site at www.ssa.gov provides excellent information in an easy-to-understand format.

BREAKING EVEN

Once we've considered the non-financial factors in retirement, we must weigh the financial benefits of early vs. late retirement.

There are several considerations in determining how long it will take to break even financially if you wait until later to retire. Cost of living, return on investment, and inflation all factor in, but most people feel that the "break even" age is seventy-seven. If you wait until sixty-five to start receiving benefits, you must live beyond seventy-seven to have made the right financial decision.

It becomes obvious then that the major consideration is: "How long do I expect to live?"

First, women outlive men. A 65-year-old woman has a remaining life expectancy of almost twenty years. A 65-year-old man's life expectancy is another fifteen years. When trying to estimate your life expectancy, consider all the factors. Do you smoke? Do you have a chronic disease? Did you care for your body in earlier years? What is your family's life expectancy? Be careful not to fall into the trap of being overly impressed by the longevity of one or two members of your family. We tend to remember our relatives with long life spans and not those with short ones. Or we concentrate on one side of the family (your mother's or father's side of the family) and forget about the others. "My grandmother on my mom's side of the family lived to be one hundred!" has to be tempered with "but my grandfather on my dad's side died at fifty-two."

SHOULD I WAIT UNTIL AFTER SIXTY-FIVE?

You do not have to start taking Social Security benefits at age sixty-five. And if you put off collecting beyond age sixty-five, you will receive more than the "full benefit" available at sixty-five. If you wait, your payments will increase by 6% for each year of delay. That's in addition to the annual cost of living adjustment. By 2008, that increase will rise to 8%.

Again, your decision to retire later has to be weighed against the same considerations as retiring early. If you enjoy working, are in good health, want to build a larger retirement nest egg or feel that you have a long life expectancy, you may consider delaying your Social Security beyond age sixty-five.

SPECIAL CONSIDERATIONS

Women must make their decisions about retirement based on different data than men. According to the Mutual Fund Education Alliance:

- Women earned only 77% of what men earned in 1999.
- Close to half of all women rely on savings and investments to meet current expenses.
- The average age of widowhood in the United States is 56.
- More than 58% of female baby boomers have less than $10,000 saved in a formal retirement plan.
- Nearly 70% of women say they have no idea how much money they'll need for retirement.
- The average woman spends 15% of her working life out of the paid

workforce caring for children and parents. For each of these years, she must work five extra years to recoup lost income, pension coverage, and career promotion.

• Women change jobs more frequently than men.

• At some point in their lives, 90% of women will be solely responsible for their finances.

This information, coupled with the fact that on the average women live several years longer than men, should help women who are considering retirement make a more informed decision about their retirement date.

One bit of good news for the divorced person — male or female: If you were married for at least ten years, you may be eligible for Social Security benefits based on your former spouse's earnings regardless of how long you have been divorced. Even if your former spouse remarries, these benefits are available. In the event of remarriage, where each marriage lasts at least ten years, all spouses can receive benefits, and one does not diminish the benefit of the other.

WHEN SHOULD I APPLY FOR SOCIAL SECURITY?

The first thing to remember is that you must request your Social Security benefits. They do not begin automatically. Three months before you plan on receiving the benefits, you should visit your local Social Security office and complete the necessary paperwork. You can call (800) 772-1213 to set up an appointment at your local Social Security office.

This is also a good time to apply for your Medicare benefits, since you can apply at the same office.

8

HOW TO INVEST
IN RETIREMENT

Doctors invest in the wildest things! Less than two years ago I received a phone call from a client who had, over the years, become a good friend. He had just completed a weekend seminar we taught on debt reduction and wealth accumulation. He was excited to tell me about an investment opportunity that was providing astonishing returns. A company from Australia had contacted him about investing in repackaged cosmetics. They explained that the cost to manufacture cosmetics and perfumes was extremely low and that repackaging the cosmetics in a more attractive style could increase their value tenfold. They would use his money to purchase the cosmetics in large quantities from the manufacturer, repackage it, and sell it at the new fee. I tried to discourage him from this type of investing, but he would hear nothing of it. He had invested with them four times and had received between 35% and 100% return within 2½ months in every case! Now they were looking for new investors.

Of course, my first response was, "When a business deal sounds too good to be true, it probably is." I asked him if he had actually received the money back on investments. He said he had. He asked my permission to have his investment advisor from Australia give me a call. The call came within two hours. And sure enough, they had an "investment" very similar to the first investment my client had made. Invest $2,500 and receive over $5,000 back in a matter of four weeks. Now, some scams are quite covert, but others you can smell more than a mile away. In this case the odor reached all the way *from Australia!*

As soon as I got off the phone, I related the incident to our CFO, who tends to do a little of his personal investing "on the fringe." We sat there trying to figure out the exact scam, and came to the conclusion that in order to gain the confidence of the investors, the company simply returned about two times the amount of their initial investment. Then as the investor moved into significantly larger investments, the company would just "hold the money in his account" and ask them to send additional money to complete each new, larger investment.

Then, the conversation turned to "Is there any way to scam the scammer?" Sure, it would be easy. Make our initial investment or two and then quit while we were ahead. We each anted up half and invested $2,500. Sure enough, within four weeks we received a check for $5,200. Four days later, we received another call from Australia, they had another excellent investment deal available for us. We would receive over 100% return on our money in just three months. The minimum investment was $15,000.

We called our client and asked him what was the biggest amount he had received back from the company. He told us it was just a little over $30,000. Armed with that information, we felt safe enough to send the $15,000. After three and a half months, we received a phone call. The cosmetics had been sold and we now had in our account $32,000. Coincidentally, they happened to have an investment available that would return 80% in six months. The minimum investment was $100,000. They encouraged us to keep the $32,000 in the account and send another $68,000 immediately. They had to have a commitment by the end of the day and had to have the money within five days. We countered that we had a building project going on in the states and we needed the money back to use in lieu of a bridge loan. If they would return the $32,000, we would reinvest as soon as we had excess cash for this type of investment. They agreed, but the money never came. We placed several calls, but our "correspondent" had moved to a different portion of the company and was no longer in charge of our account. I called the friend who had gotten us involved with the initial investment. He was still extremely high on the company and had been investing regularly, allowing them to hold his money *in the account, and with each investment, sending more money to meet the minimum investment requirements of the various deals. He had now invested just under a quarter of a million dollars! Again, I warned him about the investment, but he had total confidence. I explained to him that we could not get our $32,000 returned. He said he would put in a personal call to the company. Sure enough, in eight days we received our $32,000! Apparently they did not want to disappoint our friend. After all, they probably feel he's good for a few more rounds of investment! As for the CFO and me, we were elated to get the $32,000 check.*

HOW ARE YOU GOING TO INVEST IN RETIREMENT?

Maybe a story like the one above is a bad way to start a chapter on investing wisely. It was certainly a departure from the ordinary! But it shows how we can get carried away by non-traditional investments and scams. As we enter retirement our investment decisions become even more important. We will no longer have an opportunity to replenish savings that were lost in bad investments.

In over twenty years of working with doctors it's been my experience that doctors are lousy investors! This is due in part to the fact that they are high income individuals and if they lose money on an investment can simply go back to the well and get more money where they found their first investment monies. In retirement, however, regardless of your past earning capacity, that opportunity is no longer available.

INVESTMENT MISTAKES IN RETIREMENT

Doctors aren't the only bad investors. Many retired people make serious investment mistakes, too.

Bad Investment Mix

In our early years as investors, we can assume more risk. We can ride the wild rides of biotechnology and Internet stocks. But as we move into retirement (and even five years before retirement), we need to move into less volatile investment vehicles like Blue Chip stocks and bonds.

A five-hundred point drop on the NASDAQ could decimate a retirement account with bad allocations.

Company Stock

Some retirees have worked for the same company for forty years and have been given/earned significant amounts of company stock. In some cases their investment portfolio is made up of nearly 100% company stock. As you move into retirement, you must balance your portfolio. You are not a traitor if you cash in your company's stock — you're a wise investor.

Overly Secure

While some retired investors have a high-risk portfolio, other retirees — usually because of a lack of investment knowledge — have investments that provide so much security they barely keep up with inflation. It's not uncommon to see retirees with 70% of their investments in Certificates of Deposit (CDs). If a CD pays a 4% return and inflation is 5% for the year, the net value of your assets has actually gone down.

Unbalanced Portfolios

Many retirees feel that they have invested correctly. They have 50% of their money in stocks and 50% of their money in bonds. But over a period of time, a good stock market can create a portfolio imbalance. For example, if a retiree in 1995 would have split his retirement account evenly between stocks and bonds, because of strong stock market gains, he would have entered 2000 with 71% of his portfolio in stocks. Each year you should revisit your investment portfolio to see if you have maintained proper balance.

New Business Investing

Some people wait all their lives to own their own businesses. Upon reaching retirement age they promptly quit their jobs, apply for Social

Security, and drain their retirement accounts to invest in the startup businesses they have always wanted. Be extremely careful not to invest too much money in a startup business. Having a second career is wonderful. Sacrificing your savings to get it is not.

Over Trading

Internet trading is one of the best things that happened to investors in the last century. It allows everyone more information on investing and the ability to buy and sell investments at deeply discounted transaction prices. Internet trading is also one of the worst things that happened to investors in the last century. Today everyone's an investment genius! Why go to a casino? You can gamble away thousands of dollars just by staying home and investing online.

Don't get me wrong — I'm not against online investing — in fact, I love it! However, the thrill of the trade has to be tempered with the logic of the investment. Excess trading creates two problems. First, regardless of how low your trading fee is, you still have to pay it. And second, cashing in investments that are held for less than one year qualifies them to be taxed as ordinary income instead of long-term capital gains.

Spreading Investments Too Thinly

Many retirees will find that they opened a new retirement investment account every time they had a little extra money. As a result, some retirees have literally 15 to 20 small retirement accounts. Having too many retirement accounts creates extra cost, extra paperwork, and the need for more sophisticated money management skills — something that many older retirees do not have. If you find your retirement savings spread throughout too many accounts, you may want to consider consolidating those accounts so that they are more easily managed. If you decided to consolidate accounts, be sure that you do it in a way that does not trigger penalties or taxes.

Scam Artists

What age population is most susceptible to scam artists? Everybody knows. It's the senior citizen. I can just envision a retirement home where the residents are sitting around saying, "Drugs! No matter how much we talk to the young people about it, they still seem to become victims. They are so foolish." A few miles away in a university class-room a group of young people is saying, "Scams! No matter how much we talk to the old people about it, they still seem to become victims. They are so foolish."

It's true. No matter how often senior citizens are warned, they still fall prey to the scam. I talked to one seventy-year-old, highly-educated man who, on the advice of another retiree, invested $2,500 with an online company which was headquartered in another country. When his receipt came back, it said, "Thanks for playing the game." After a few months, he was notified by e-mail that the company had not been set up correctly and all the money was lost — but now they were set up correctly and he could reinvest! Which he did!

Investing Before Retirement

Investing, whether before or after retirement, is a complicated and ongoing process. And while we should learn all we can about investing, a vast majority of us will never have nearly as much knowledge as pro-fessional investors. As a result, it behooves each of us to have profes-sional financial advisors, which may include an attorney, accountant and financial planner. Your retirement planning requires the input of the big boys.

If you still have several years before retirement, make the best of it.

Make Full Use of Tax-Deferred Accounts

To encourage Americans to save for their own retirement, the fed-eral government offers tax-advantaged types of retirement accounts and savings plans. They include traditional IRAs, 401(k) plans, 403(b) plans, SIMPLE plans, SEP plans, KEOGH plans and fixed and variable annuities. Talk with your financial advisor and decide which account is available and best for you. Then, begin maximizing that account on an annual basis by investing early each year.

Investment Mix

As a rule, if retirement is still a long way off, you will want at least 60% of your assets in equities. As you near retirement, you will need to start locking up your funds in safer securities, such as bonds. Many financial consultants recommend up to 50% of your portfolio in bonds once you reach retirement. The Standard & Poors Corporation has created a model portfolio for three hypothetical investors: a 30-year old, a 45-year old, and a 55-year old. As you can see from figure 8.1, early investing will be basically all stocks with a predominance in large cap stock. As time goes on, bonds become more important. At retirement, they suggest 50% of the portfolio in bonds.

Each investor has a different risk tolerance. Those with a low risk tolerance will want more secure investments but may sacrifice a higher return on investment. Figure 8.2 shows various asset allocations relative to risk. Retirees with a high-risk tolerance or those who must attempt to get the maximum return on investment may want to continue to invest up to 65% of their retirement portfolio in stocks.

Today, there are investment funds specifically designed for investors expecting to retire at various ages. These fund managers do all the allocation for you by investing in different stock, bond and cash funds. This means that they are actually funds made up of other funds. This type of fund may be the solution for your asset allocation concerns but does come at a price. Most funds of this type charge a fee on top of those fees already charged by the underlying funds.

FIG. 8.1

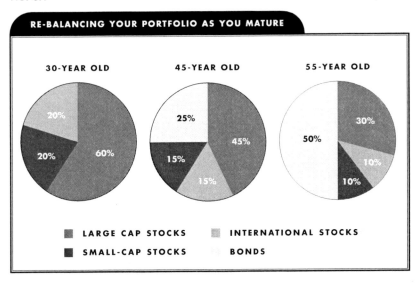

RE-BALANCING YOUR PORTFOLIO AS YOU MATURE

30-YEAR OLD   45-YEAR OLD   55-YEAR OLD

- LARGE CAP STOCKS   INTERNATIONAL STOCKS
- SMALL-CAP STOCKS   BONDS

FIG. 8.2

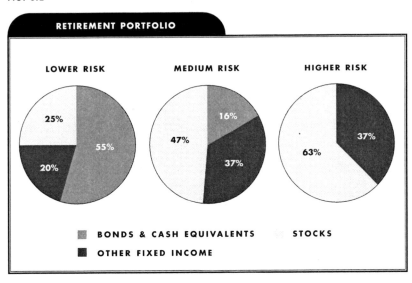

RETIREMENT PORTFOLIO

LOWER RISK   MEDIUM RISK   HIGHER RISK

- BONDS & CASH EQUIVALENTS   STOCKS
- OTHER FIXED INCOME

UNDERSTANDING VARIOUS INVESTMENTS

Everyone should seek professional help with their retirement plans — especially in the areas of investment, asset protection and taxes. By the same token, no one is as interested in your retirement as you! As a result, you need to have a basic knowledge of investing.

Stocks

Today in America over 40% of households own stocks in a publicly traded company. These stocks may be in a single company or stocks from a group of companies combined into one fund called a mutual fund. Historically, only stocks have provided enough long-term growth to keep ahead of inflation. That's why once you have retired, stocks should still be a significant part of your portfolio. Stocks are classified as either large cap stocks or small cap stocks. Determining the size of a stock is relatively simple. Its current price per share multiplied by the number of outstanding shares will tell you the size of the stock. If the total is one billion dollars or less, it is a small cap stock. Everything above one billion dollars qualifies as a large cap stock. In general, small cap stocks provide a better return than large cap stocks, but their price swings are much greater. As a result, most financial advisors encourage large cap stocks in the stock portion of your portfolio once you reach retirement. You can also create more security in the stock portion of your portfolio by investing in large cap stocks that are from non-related classes. For example, investing in General Motors and IBM may provide more security than investing in two automobile manufacturers, like General Motors and Ford.

Today, a common way of investing in the stock market is through index funds. An index fund is a stock mutual fund that owns all the stock in a popular stock index. For instance, the Standard & Poors 500 Index contains 500 large stocks. The index fund owns those 500 stocks in the same proportion as the S & P 500 Index. You can create even more diversity in your index fund by using funds like the Schwab 1000 or Wilshire 5000 Funds.

The advantage of a mutual fund is that you've spread your risk and have nearly mirrored the growth of the market. The disadvantage is that since you have matched the market, you will never outperform the market. But don't be too concerned. Index funds generally do better than 80% of all large company stock funds over the long term. They also do better than 80% of all the stock money managers, better than 80% of all stock pension funds, and better than 80% of the stock recommendations of all the stock gurus writing newsletters. This has been true in the 1970s, the 1980s, and the 1990s. It is true when the stock market goes up, down, or remains flat. This is due in part to the fact that index funds have a lower management fee in that the stocks are selected simply by formula to reflect the definition of the fund.

Bonds

Our need for bonds in retirement is simple — security. Bonds will dampen the volatility created by the stock in your portfolio. While you can invest in individual bonds, you may prefer to invest in bond funds as long as they reflect your investment goals.

The disadvantage of a bond-heavy retirement portfolio is that a bond paying 5% barely keeps ahead of the current 3-4% inflation rate. If inflation rises rapidly, your bonds or bond funds may not be able to keep up.

Variable Annuities

Variable annuities guarantee you a monthly payment for life, but have a fairly high annual fee — 2.1% on the average — and surrender charges of 6-9%. As a result, variable annuities make sense only if: (1) you have ten or more years before retirement; (2) you have made maximum contributions to all tax-deferred plans, including IRAs, 401(k), and the employer's pension plan; (3) you have additional funds to invest; and (4) you want retirement income you won't outlive.

Real Estate

Real estate can be an excellent retirement asset, but it's not for everyone. It may be logical to have real estate investments in your retirement portfolio if:

- You owned real estate as part of your business before retiring and the new business owners prefer to lease this real estate so they can continue to house the business in its same location.

- You have spent your pre-retirement years in the real estate business. If you understand and enjoy real estate and are in good health, the management of your real estate can be a good part-time job and increase your ROI through sweat equity.

- You have real estate that is in a location that will cause appreciation now and in the near future.

- You have a long-term, AAA rated tenant as the leasee.

- You can expect a predictable total return of 10% or more per year.

- Low-cost management is available if outsourcing is necessary.

- You have owned a real estate prior to retirement and have a low cost basis in the property which could result in a large tax consequence upon the sale of the property.

If your real estate investing does not meet these criteria, you may consider rolling those investments into less management intensive assets.

9
WHERE ARE WE GOING TO RETIRE?

Dr. Conrad started his professional life as a veterinarian. He then sold his practice and went back to school to become a chiropractor. Now, he's ready to retire from his chiropractic practice as well, and knows exactly what he wants to do with his time in retirement. Winters will be spent as a fishing guide in Brazil and summers will be spent as a fishing guide in Alaska. To him, that's retirement at its best. Unfortunately, his wife doesn't agree. It seems that many times our retirement dreams and our retirement realities take two different paths.

WHERE ARE YOU GOING TO LIVE?

Only *you* can decide where *you* want to retire. For some, it's a foregone conclusion. "I was born here, lived here and will die here," or "All the kids live around here and there's no reason to move," or "Most of our friends here in the North moved to Sarasota and we're just waiting until Jack retires to join them."

Many of us look forward to the move after retirement. About 30% of all Americans move at some point after retirement. That includes 4% who move out of their home state. And those numbers are increasing. Our surveys show that 53% of working professionals plan on moving after retirement. Right now, Henderson, Nevada, is the single hottest retirement spot in the nation. According to some retirees, there should be pearly gates at the entrance to the city. But Henderson isn't the only land of retirement opportunity. Perhaps the best book ever written on retirement locations is *Retirement Places Rated* by David Savageau. In it he rates the top thirty retirement places in America using a somewhat sophisticated but easy-to-understand rating system. As you might expect, various cities in Arizona and Florida are among the favorites, and then, of course, there is Henderson — right near the top again! Even if you don't choose one of Savageau's top thirty places, the book is an excellent reference for determining the ideal retirement spot.

Taxes

According to the book *Citizen Hughes*, Howard Hughes, one of the richest men in the world, lived in Nevada in large part because there was no state tax. Taxes in retirement contribute greatly to the cost of living. A couple retiring in Henderson, Nevada, with an annual retirement income of $70,000, can save several thousand dollars per year in taxes when compared to many other retirement areas.

States like Alaska, Florida, Nevada, South Dakota, Texas, Washington, and Wyoming have no state income tax. Other states, such as Alabama, Hawaii, Illinois, Mississippi, New Hampshire, Pennsylvania, and Tennessee have some form of income tax, but do not tax retirement income. States including Arkansas, Colorado, Delaware, Indiana, Louisiana, Maryland, Michigan, Montana, New Jersey, North Carolina, Oregon, South Carolina, Utah, Virginia, and West Virginia give partial tax breaks if you are at or near sixty-five years old. My wife and I have residences in Florida, Nebraska, and Oklahoma. In the past, we could have made a good case that our legal domicile is either Nebraska or Oklahoma — but not Florida. Unfortunately, both Nebraska and Oklahoma (along with Arizona, California, Connecticut, Georgia, Idaho, Indiana, Iowa, Kansas, Kentucky, Maine, Massachusetts, Minnesota, Missouri, New Mexico, North Dakota, Rhode Island, Vermont and Wisconsin) give no special tax treatment to retirement income. As we enter more full-time retirement, we may spend a majority of our time in Florida and make it our home state.

The AARP publishes a booklet entitled *Relocation Tax Guide: State Tax Information for Relocation Decisions*. This free booklet provides easy-to-understand information on a state-by-state basis.

If you have moved (or will be moving) to a tax advantaged state, you will want to establish legal domicile (where you legally live) as soon as possible. If you will live in two or more states — one with better tax advantages — you will want to establish legal domicile in that state. That's not always easy. You must be able to show proof of normal living activities in that state. Having a vacation home in Southern California that you use only during the three winter months will not qualify as legal domicile.

If your area of residence is ever questioned, the following items will help you prove your residency.

1. Where you file your taxes.
2. Where you are registered to vote.
3. The state issuing your driver's license.
4. The address on recent legal documents.
5. The address on your financial accounts and legal contracts.
6. The title and registration of vehicles.

Some states, such as Florida, provide forms for you to register your residency.

Personal Preferences

Regardless of how good a guide for rating retirement locations is, it still remains just that — a "guide" to retirement places. Your personal preferences may still outweigh any geographic, climatic or other factors. In our most recent survey, 65% of the respondents said their children or other family members would affect their decision regarding where to retire. You may want to live near your children or siblings. You may need to live near your aging parents. You may have strong ties to your church or other religious organizations or may just have a host of great friends you don't want to leave!

Even the best retirement guides rate retirement areas based on what they assume are logical preferences. But your preferences may not fit "typical." A few months ago I had the opportunity to visit a dog sled camp in the lower part of Alaska accessible only by helicopter. The camp consisted of twelve people and one-hundred-fifty dogs. The opportunity to ride on these dog sleds was incredible! I asked our musher (one of the twelve people who lived in the camp) where he went during the winter. He said he moved north twelve hundred miles to help train dogs! To each his own.

THE PERFECT SPOT

For me, the perfect retirement spot can be summed up in two words, *warm* and *water*. Put me on a shoreline with the hot sun beating down and I'm happy. You may love the four seasons, the mountains, desert or rolling hills of green vegetation. You may prefer a farm in the Midwest, a bungalow in Cape Cod or a Manhattan apartment. Let your personal preference guide you. Don't let other people decide what you want in retirement. You're old enough now to make your own decisions. Here are some other factors to consider.

Cost of Living

Cost of living indexes are made up of various items including taxes, housing, transportation, utilities and food. Different cost of living criteria will, of course, produce slightly different ratings. Again, a guide such as *Retirement Places Rated* gives by far the best synopsis.

Climate

Most people equate climate to temperature, but many factors make up climate. Areas around large bodies of water, particularly the ocean, tend to take on the characteristics of the water and will heat and cool more slowly than the inland. One of my favorite retirement spots, New Smyrna Beach, Florida, has a significantly different temperature than towns just fifteen miles inland. Areas in the higher latitudes tend to have more fluctuation and seasonal shifts in both temperature range and hours of light. Elevation can also have a large effect. States like Arizona provide cool, high elevation areas and warm, low elevation areas just a few hours apart. Wind contributes to wind chill factors and can make tolerable winter temperatures less than tolerable. Humidity also plays a major role in comfort. A temperature of ninety degrees in an arid 25% relative humidity feels like eighty-eight degrees. That same ninety-degree temperature with 55% relative humidity feels like ninety-six degrees.

This summer, when I landed in Juneau, Alaska, I completed a life-long goal of visiting all fifty states. One thing is almost universal throughout the states. Everyone feels that they have the most volatile weather and exaggerated temperature changes. Natives in every state tell visitors "we always say around here in (fill in the name of the state), if you don't like the weather, just hang around for thirty minutes 'cuz, it'll change." So when you ask the locals about the weather, be sure to temper it with the information from reliable retirement guides.

Seasonally Affected Disorder (SAD) is a condition from which some people suffer, which causes them significant depression if they are not exposed to the sun on a regular basis. Though I have no proof, I believe that many of us suffer from mild cases of SAD. And while it is perhaps psychological, you may still want to consider the number of sunny days per year of your retirement location. Good retirement guides will list the number of sunny days of each retirement location.

Terrain and Landscape

Some people like mountains, others prefer flatland. Some people prefer heavy vegetation, others prefer the dry desert look. You must decide what you like.

Altitude

The fresh air of a high altitude resort area can be invigorating, but if you suffer from altitude sickness or have heart or lung insufficiency, you may opt for lower altitudes.

Work Potential

Since many people will work in retirement, your retirement location should be rated according to the potential to find work. Most working retirees will be working part-time, so you will want to find a location that has adequate opportunity for part-time employment and is willing to work with retirement age employees.

Lifestyle

Over your lifetime you have developed a certain lifestyle. Retiring in an area that supports that lifestyle may be important to you. The residents of your retirement area will become your future friends and neighbors. If their lifestyle is similar to yours, it will make transition into the community easier and more enjoyable.

Leisure and Recreation

Leisure and recreation time will take up a large portion of your early retirement. As a result, it is an important consideration. Golf courses, jogging terrain, fishing opportunities and people with the same leisure and recreational interests can add to the enjoyment of your retirement spot.

Fine Arts

The lure of a remote mountain cabin has to be weighed against the fact that you may be miles from the closest performing arts center or museum. Almost all retirees maintain an interest in fine arts similar to what they had before retirement. If you are actively involved in the arts events of your community, you will probably want to maintain that lifestyle in retirement.

Services

In our early retirement, public services are not on the top of our priority list. As we age, certain services, such as government agencies and hospital facilities become more important. Since you will probably maintain your retirement location into later retirement, these service factors should be considered.

Culture

America is truly the land of cultural and ethnic diversity. Take into consideration the cultural make-up of the retirement community and the immediate surrounding area. Some retirees prefer multi-cultural diversity offering a variety of languages, ethnic foods, and customs. Others prefer retirement communities with people of similar ethnic backgrounds.

Crime Rate

While crime rate information is important and available for most major cities, the crime rate of your "retirement niche" in that area may vary greatly from published reports. Everyone is aware of cities that have high crime rates in certain areas and low crime rates in others. Be sure to locate in the best area available. Gated communities and home security systems also decrease your susceptibility to crime.

Friends

Where will your friends retire? Sometimes that's important in making your decision. In helping one Michigan retiree, who had worked as a guard at the penitentiary, we found an excellent retirement spot near Daytona, but he preferred the Bradenton, Florida area — because that's where all his friends were retiring.

Scouting the Area

Researching your new retirement area is probably the most enjoyable part of retirement planning. But rather than just pick up and move there, you should probably make extended visits to find out if the area is really as terrific as you think or if you've just been caught up by the "grass is always greener" syndrome.

The good news is you don't have to wait until you retire to start checking out your dreamland. Plan on making at least two visits to your potential retirement area — one during the off season. It may be a lot hotter, colder, more crowded, or more desolate than you had imagined. And even if your trip to this retirement area is vacation oriented, take time to find out the facts and understand the area. Ask a realtor to show you homes in your price range. Program yourself to think long-term. Your retirement is longer than the three days you spent on the beach. Again, think long-term. What things might change? Will the population increase dramatically and change the atmosphere of the area? Is the community at the age that buildings and homes will start deteriorating more rapidly? Is it located near a higher crime area that has potential to spread? Visit with the locals. They'll give you information that realtors and chambers of commerce aren't as willing to share.

Before you make a final decision, you may want to test retirement life in the area. Rent a home for one year; it will give you time to understand the area much better. Don't make the mistake of building your dream home before you are sure it's where you want to spend your retirement.

10

WHAT WILL THE KIDS AND SPOUSE SAY?

S everal years ago our company was trying to recruit one of the top prospects in the nation. To make it even more of a challenge, he would have to relocate from California to Nebraska! The pay was right and he wanted the job, but still had some reservations because of his close family ties. Instead of increasing the salary above what we already had, we instead decided to pay the costs of moving his retired parents to Nebraska. We also provided his brother and sister-in-law part-time work. It was enough to tilt the decision in favor of Nebraska! Sometimes it's surprising the effect your family — even your extended family — has on your life.

HAVE YOU REACHED AGREEMENT?

Just when you reach the age that you can quit worrying about what your parents think, you have to start worrying about what your kids think! Retirement planning would be easy if it happened in a vacuum — without the surrounding influences of family and friends. In many cases, however, your retirement decisions will be made by agreement with your spouse and possibly even approval of your children.

SPOUSAL ACCORD

It's said that many couples "grow together" as they age. This means that we tend to become more homogenous in our thoughts, actions and desires. But in most cases, the more closely we examine our preferences, the more differences we find. My wife and I both agree that we will spend a good portion of our retirement life in Florida. That's where the agreement stops. I want to live right on the beach. Close doesn't count. She, on the other hand, has her sights set on a beautiful home that backs onto a nature preserve. It has a screened in area equipped with a built-in grill and a hot tub with overflowing waters that cascade into the pool. Obviously, we still have some decisions to make!

APPROVAL OF THE CHILDREN

Even after you and your spouse have agreed on a retirement setting, the plan may need to be "approved" by your children. Just as you spent the first half of your life helping them, they may spend the second half of their life helping you. Long-distance relationships between parents and children can throw an extra burden on the care-giving child.

GAINING CONSENSUS

Eventually, all of your retirement questions must be answered. Decisions must be made and actions must be taken. Employing good decision-making procedures will make the process easier.

Keep an Open Mind

Who knows! Your spouse may be right — your children may have a better idea — and maybe your idea isn't so good after all. Some people tend to grow more opinionated as they grow older. Listen to your spouse and others. Try to visualize the good in their plan.

Discuss Plans Early and Often

The more we verbalize our ideas, the more vivid the plans grow. Some psychologists feel that our subconscious mind cannot tell the difference between what is real and what is vividly imagined. Spend time rehearsing your retirement in conversation. Each conversation will bring up new problems and solutions. Eventually, the plan will take on a definite form.

Visit Your Retirement Location

If a picture is worth a thousand words, then a visit is worth a thousand pictures. Many of your problems will melt away once you visit a few of your choice retirement areas. Again, be sure to spend enough time so you get more than a vacationer's view of the area.

Find Common Ground

I want the beach; she wants a house with a beautiful screened-in area. Perhaps we should look for a house on the beach with a beautiful screened-in area! If, as a couple, you find yourself at an impasse, create a new positive outlook by listing all of the retirement criteria you have in common. You both like a certain state, you both want a warm climate, you're both interested in a gated community with common area maintenance, and you both like an open house design. Visiting your similarities sometimes helps overcome your differences.

Compromise a Little

Some decisions that seem important at the time fade very rapidly. One retirement couple got into a bitter argument over the color of grout to be used between the tile in their new entryway. Hey, we're retirement age; it's too late in life to sweat the small stuff.

Do Both

Remember the old pizza commercial that starred Dion Sanders? In the commercial, Dallas Cowboys owner Jerry Jones asked multi-talented Dion Sanders what he preferred to play, baseball or football. Dion answered, "Both." "Okay," Jerry said, "If you play football, what do you prefer to play, offense or defense?" Dion again answered, "Both." At the end of the commercial, Jerry Jones asked, "And what salary do you want four million — or six million?" To which Dion answers, "Both!"

Maybe you can have your cake and eat it too. Think creatively. If your spouse prefers an Ozark retirement setting and you prefer a condo on the beach, perhaps a permanent home in the Ozarks and a two-month time share or annual two-month rental on the beach during the winter will satisfy both of you.

There are lots of exciting decisions in front of you. Enjoy the trip.

11

YOUR HOME
OR HOMES

Everyone has a slightly different opinion of the perfect home. Mine has changed several times over the decades.

After living in a few starter homes, I decided what I really wanted was a quiet home away from the frenzied pace of a busy practice. I searched for about a year and finally found the ideal location — a totally secluded country estate over a quarter mile from the nearest public road. Huge stone pillars and swinging iron gates guarded the entrance off the road. The private drive was tree-lined and dropped steeply into a ravine — across a bridge — and rose steeply again until the trees stopped at the edge of a grassy meadow. On one side was an area for playing games, and on the other side was a tennis court. The drive rose steeply again, through hundreds of cedar trees, stopping at the top of the hill as a circular drive in front of our home. The back of the home had a swimming pool and adjoining hot tub. Just beyond the hot tub, the bluff dropped off sharply to an area that was once used as a grass airstrip. The inside of the home took on a rustic cabin look. Indeed I had found my place away from the city.

Over time, I left private practice and moved into full-time consulting. Now I had no patient contact and only occasional contact with clients. The need for seclusion quickly evaporated and was replaced by the desire for some of the amenities that we left back in the city. The closest Dairy Queen was now seven miles away, the grocery store five miles, and church ten. The rains of the spring and the snows of the winter sometimes left roads impassable and added to our inability to get to the city as much as we wanted. And then there were those little "varmints" that always visit country homes when the weather turns cold. Before long it became apparent that we were city dwellers living in the country.

Almost in a knee-jerk reaction we moved from the country to the ultimate city home. Actually, it was more than a home. The same family had occupied this mansion since it was built in 1908. Everyone from U.S. Presidents to movie stars had visited it. J. Sterling Morton, the founder of Arbor Day, had planned its grounds. It was four stories, not counting the huge fallout shelter. The plaster crown molding on the main floor had been flown in from Western Europe, the tile from Italy, and its lead-framed windows are unseen in today's architecture. It had ten bathrooms, a large pool totally enclosed by glass, a few spas, and a twenty-person sauna. Hidden passageways, servants quarters (which we turned into a play room), commercial heaters for the outdoor patio, and an outdoor slate entrance created the perfect utopia — at least for a time.

Over a period of time, things changed! I was now at a point in my professional career when I could afford to take extended vacations. The children were growing up, and the wonderful amenities of living in a mansion were now being offset by the reality of its costs. A home built in 1908 needs upkeep; utility bills in an older home are much higher. One month, our handyman, in an effort to dry some sheet rock repair on the fourth floor, turned the thermostat to 80 degrees. Since we never used the fourth floor we were rather surprised when our monthly utility bill for heating alone was $1,600! There were lots of other hidden costs, too. Now instead of having a housekeeper once a week, it became once a week — per floor. But perhaps the final realization occurred when I found myself home alone one night for about two hours before I heard a noise and realized that my family was home — just on a different floor and in a different part of the house! I was ready to try something different.

We downsized homes, but because I now had more free time and teenage kids, a second home on the lake sounded good. We soon built a beautiful home on a 400-acre lake. The ceilings in the great room were 28-feet high and the entire lakeside was windows. The lowest level of this three-story lake house was used as our recreation area. The fourteen-foot-high ceilings made it great for basketball — with a nine-foot hoop. Outdoor fun included a sandlot volleyball court, a huge dock for fishing and boating, and all the water toys including a pontoon boat, fishing boat, and jetski. It was the perfect getaway; my wife and I could go by ourselves or invite friends.

Before long, some of my wife's older relatives, who lived in Tulsa, started to need more help from the family. We also had good friends we missed in the Tulsa area where she had grown up. Before we knew it, we had purchased another home in Tulsa — this time a modest, two-bedroom, two-garage patio-home in a gated community. We enjoyed the Tulsa home, but it led us to our next realization — for a couple not yet totally retired, three homes is more than enough! And since our lake home was an hour's drive from our primary residence, we decided we would offer it for sale. It sold almost immediately.

Some things learned in life you learn the simple way — by reading a book or observing other people's experiences. Other things you learn the hard way — through your own experiences. In the case of finding the right home, I feel I have used the latter technique.

WHERE DO YOU WANT TO LIVE?

As you enter retirement you have to make a significant decision. What will your retirement home look like? As you might expect, a vast majority of people prefer to retire in the home in which they are currently living. In fact, a survey in 1990 indicated that 86% of the then-current retirees preferred to stay in their pre-retirement homes. On the other hand, a lot has changed in the last ten to fifteen years. Many people are retiring closer to age fifty than sixty. As a result, some pre-retirees are favoring a more far-sighted strategy. They are looking for vacation homes they can enjoy now and retire in later. Another option is downsizing (or upsizing) to a new retirement home. Still others plan to have more than one home in retirement. So the number of people that will move to a new home in retirement continues to grow.

STAYING IN YOUR PRESENT HOME

There are a lot of advantages to staying in your present home. First, there's a good chance that your friends and family now live around you. If you relocate it will mean establishing new friendships and may mean moving away from the family. You are also ingrained into the community in many other ways. You understand how it's laid out, where the grocery stores are and where the best shopping is. You have established relationships with your church, bank, doctor, and other community businesses. Financial considerations include the cost savings from not having to relocate, the fact that your mortgage may now be paid off, and that you are accustomed to your current property taxes. Selling a home and relocating may come with unforeseen costs including a five to seven percent realtor's fee, closing fees, and financing fees on a new home. Plus, there are typical new home needs, such as window coverings, appliances, towel bars, storage shelves, and all the other things not included in a new home.

DISADVANTAGES OF STAYING PUT

Would you be willing to give me $100,000 of your retirement nest egg if I did not return it to your estate until after your death and with very little or no interest? Probably not, but that's in essence what occurs when you continue to live in an oversized house. Downsizing may free up thousands of dollars that can be added to your income retirement fund to start drawing interest.

Other factors may also make moving your best choice. If your home is too large, you are paying utility bills, taxes and upkeep that could be avoided if you moved to a smaller home. Is the neighborhood deteriorating? Are there impending tax hikes or community improvement assessments that could increase your cost of living? And is your home of the age that it will need repairs as you're entering your retirement years?

BUYING A NEW HOME FOR RETIREMENT

If you decide to buy a new home, perhaps the most important question is, "How much home do I need?" In the last few decades, many people financed their retirements, in part, by downsizing their homes. Big homes that were purchased thirty or forty years ago are now mortgage free and have appreciated substantially. Downsizing allowed the retiree to move into a new, smaller home, debt-free and with money left over to add to the retirement nest egg. But downsizing may not be the panacea that it appears. It's one thing to spend a few weeks in a vacation bungalow, but another thing to move all of your possessions into a smaller home that will become your full-time residence.

If a new home is in your retirement future, think long-term. Is your retirement home:

Barrier free

While you may still be running or playing tennis on a regular basis, there may come a time when steps, entryways with thresholds, narrow hallways, and multiple living levels create problems. Wide doorways, banisters, and covered entryways may also become important.

Convenient

Convenience comes in many different forms. An oversized garage is nice for the older driver, and automatic garage door openers become more important. Adequate phone jacks and computer connections throughout the house are important for the person who will work from their home part-time during retirement.

Secure

Adequate outdoor lighting, security systems and even gated communities can add to your security in retirement. An attached garage offers both convenience and security since it allows you to move from your home to your car without going outside and without the worry of inclement weather.

Efficient

Zoned heating and air conditioning, ceiling fans, and energy efficient design and construction will provide long-term efficiency and reduce the size of utility bills. Chances are you'll live in this home long enough to recoup all the additional construction cost via lower utility bills.

BUYING A PRE-EXISTING HOME

Some retirees will want the opportunity to build their own retirement dream homes, but many will avoid the stresses of building by purchasing existing homes. Before you purchase an existing home, be sure you answer the following questions:

• *Is this a well-built home?* Some contractors try to provide too much home for the money by sacrificing quality throughout the home. Insulation, plumbing fixtures, appliances and floor coverings come in many different grades. Be sure your home has been built with adequate quality.

• *Can I personalize my residence?* Many retirement homes are in planned communities. These planned communities are often intentionally created with a uniform look. House color, yard ornaments and even landscape plans may need to be approved by the homeowners association. Be sure you can live with the rules of the association.

• *Will I have a private outdoor area?* Today, patio homes are becoming very popular as retirement residences. A patio home is usually built in a planned community where all grounds upkeep is provided by the association. In patio home communities, each home has a small, enclosed outdoor area that can be used as the homeowner sees fit. This allows for lawn chairs, outdoor grills, chimeneas, birdfeeders, flowers and other personal, outdoor decorating.

• *Is the home barrier free?* Again, steps, entrance thresholds, narrow hallways and small bathrooms can be a problem for retirees in later life.

• *Is the residence close enough to the main shopping areas, grocery stores, recreation areas, churches and other community activities?* Is it located within a reasonable distance of other family members who may help you in your retirement years?

• *Does the home provide adequate privacy?* Houses built too close together or common areas adjacent to your residence may prevent privacy. If the community is being built, be sure that future building will not erode your current privacy.

• *Can I continue to maintain my pets, hobbies, and activities while living in this new retirement home?* Be sure you can maintain the lifestyle you want.

MORE THAN ONE HOME

Owning two or more homes is a growing trend among retirees. In a recent survey of professionals, 38% said they planned to split time between two residences. They see the opportunity to double their pleasure by spending part of their year in one home and the rest of the year in another. This can be accomplished in several ways. Many empty-nesters decide to trade down to a smaller, primary residence and then use the profit to purchase a second home. Others keep their current home and simply buy a second one.

Not every home has to be a freestanding house. Your second home may be an apartment style home in a high-rise, a condo in a resort area or a patio home in a warm weather retirement community. In some instances, even a time-share will satisfy your desire for a second home. The second home may also help the couple who has different ideas on retirement to live in harmony! For the couple where the wife wants to continue to live in the North near the grandchildren, and the husband hates the cold and wants to retire South where it's warm, a second home may be the perfect solution. That way the couple lives in the North near their family during the summer and in the warm, sunny South during the winter.

LOCATING YOUR SECOND HOME

Perhaps everyone has a slightly different opinion as to where their second retirement home should be located. Many people prefer a second home in or near a resort area. Whether it's Cape Cod or the Ozarks, resort areas provide a certain excitement in retirement. On the other hand, some people prefer retirement homes that are off the beaten path. This allows the retiree to enjoy the area without paying full price. For years, New Smyrna Beach, Florida, had limited access because of the poor road system and bridges between the mainland and the beach. This has since been corrected in the last decades. The beaches of New Smyrna have the same beauty as those in Daytona Beach, just a few miles north. But because New Smyrna is off the beaten path, the price of a retirement home can be significantly less than homes on the beach in other areas of the state.

In some cases, you may choose to have your second home in the area that was once your primary living area. A Detroit couple may be able to stay close to family and friends by buying their second home in the community in which they lived and worked prior to retirement and have their primary home in a resort area.

Our interviews with a wide variety of retirees made obvious the fact that even if you plan to retire in a more rural area, you will want to be near a larger city. The needs for health care, discount shopping, and air travel make areas near larger cities a better buy.

BUYING EARLY

More and more couples are buying their second home several years before retiring. They figure they can enjoy it now as a vacation home and later as a retirement home. Others feel that homes in resort areas will continue to appreciate and want to buy now to avoid getting locked out of the market because of inflation.

If you plan on having a second retirement home, you may want to rent a home in that community for a few seasons before purchasing. This will allow you to become more familiar with the community and just taste retirement life in general. It will also allow you to study the market and wait for a good buy — perhaps during the off-season.

DISADVANTAGES OF A SECOND HOME

While it's appealing to think of having two homes, there are significant disadvantages.

Double Upkeep

The purchase price of a second home is only a portion of the total additional costs. There are three other types of expenses to consider in owning a second home. The first is the "ongoing" expense. Electricity, garbage, phone, other utilities and maintenance will be ongoing. The second type of expense will generally occur once, or will not reoccur for several years, such as buying window coverings, furniture and landscape items. The last type of expense, expendable items, such as laundry detergent and personal grooming items, will be needed regardless of which residence you are at. These expendable items add very little to the cost of maintaining a second home.

Concern

While caught up in the excitement of buying a second home, it's important to remember that there will be additional responsibility and concern. The couple who lives in Minnesota now has more need for concern when a hurricane is approaching their vacation home on the Gulf Coast. You receive a call from the security company; your alarm has been activated in your second home — 1,000 miles away. It could be a false alarm, but then, it may be an intruder. The weather forecast says the coldest spot in the nation is right where your second home is located. The possibility of frozen pipes can be unsettling.

If you will be leaving one house unoccupied for a very long period of time, lots of things can go wrong. Insurance companies realize this, too. Many companies charge higher premiums, sometimes up to 50% more, for part-time homes.

A Busy Lifestyle

Your lifestyle will be more complicated simply because you have two residences. Your planner now not only lists what you have to do today, but also where you will be today. You will be getting mail at two different addresses, need to set up two sets of doctors and perhaps even license vehicles in two different states.

Distance Between Homes

Be careful not to let your dream for a vacation/retirement home force you into bad decisions. Buying a retirement dream home while you are still working full-time may not allow you to use that dream home with any frequency. In addition, buying a second home which is a long distance from your first home may prevent you from using the second home as you had planned.

OTHER SOLUTIONS

Not everyone that wants a second home needs a full-time second home. Some couples prefer to share ownership in a second home. One retiree considered buying a second home in Florida with a younger couple. The young couple had children and could use the home only during the summer when school was out. The retired couple would use the house during the winter months. It created an excellent relationship. Time-shares or renting a home "for the season" may also satisfy your desire for a second home.

RENTING YOUR SECOND HOME

The strong demand for vacation rentals may make owning a second home more affordable. In many resort areas, you can count on a stream of rental income to offset a large portion of your ongoing home costs. If you decide that you will be renting your second home, you may want to consider an apartment or condo since they rent more easily than houses. Even if you do not plan on renting your second home on a regular basis, you may want to rent it occasionally throughout the year. The IRS allows you to rent your home income tax free if you rent it for fewer than 15 days per year. If you rent for 15 days or more, however, you must report the income.

You will want to make your decision about renting your second residence before applying for a loan on the residence. Most lending institutions will give you a mortgage for 90% of the home price if you are buying the home for your personal use (or it's rented less than 15 days per year). If you plan on using your second home as a rental property for 15 days or more, lenders will ask for a 20% down payment. The interest rate may also be slightly higher.

SELLING YOUR SECOND HOME

While the dream of owning a second home is exciting in early retirement, it usually gives way to the desire of a simpler life in later retirement years. As a result, many people will want to sell their second home in later retirement. And while this can sometimes be a burden, it also serves to free up money to use in later retirement.

12
YOUR MISSION

J erry has worked all his life as a mechanic. In high school he heard that automatic transmission mechanics could make up to ten dollars per hour, and when he was young that was a big wage! As soon as he completed high school he enrolled in technical college, but soon changed his career path from automatic transmission repair to automotive mechanic. Upon graduation he took a job in a five-man garage and soon found that while the garage did indeed charge ten dollars per hour for his work, he received only four dollars per hour. After several years as an employee Jerry decided to try it on his own. He had plenty of business and was busy from dawn until dusk, but found that redoing jobs that weren't done right the first time, running for parts, and doing book-work — coupled with normal overhead expenses — still netted only a modest wage. He had become somewhat disillusioned with his chosen profession. In fact, he found most of his enjoyment came from public speaking — something he had done since early high school years. He was good at it and was frequently paid as much for a one-hour speech as he made during an entire day as a mechanic.

Tired of the extra work and overhead involved with self-employment, and looking for a little more security now that he was in his mid-forties, he took a job for a large company maintaining their fleet of service vehicles. Even though the hours were shorter, the job was easier and he received better pay, he soon realized that his love affair with the automobile was long over.

Today, in his late fifties, he realizes his first love is — and always will be — public speaking! He also realizes that he is just three years away from early *retirement. And if he expects to be on the speaking circuit in three years, he has to "ramp up" right now.*

His new vision has given him new energy. He's busy preparing speeches, making contacts, updating promotional material, and renewing old contacts. Retirement has provided him an opportunity to pursue the dream not available during his forty years as a mechanic.

YOUR MISSION IN RETIREMENT

What are you going to do when you grow up — the whole way up — into retirement? Some people are fortunate enough to spend their entire working career in what they believe was their ultimate calling. For others, the job was just that — a job, and not necessarily fulfilling. Perhaps you lost interest in your profession because of changes in the profession, changes in your thinking, physical stresses or other unforeseen changes that have occurred over the last thirty to forty years. Perhaps your job was fine, as jobs go, but you feel a more important calling which can only be accomplished once you reach retirement. For you, retirement will take on a new excitement. You will have new vitality. You will become a different person. For you, the opportunity to serve on a mission field, start a second career, complete your bachelor's degree or become the public speaker you always dreamed of being will make retirement the happiest time of your life!

GOALS IN RETIREMENT

Maybe you were lucky and had the opportunity to fulfill your life's mission through your occupation. That doesn't mean excitement doesn't await you in retirement. Even people like Michael Jordan, who felt they completed their mission (six NBA championships) before retirement, find that they need future goals to remain happy in retirement. Your goals may be as simple as creating adequate time to babysit your grandchildren or as unique as starting your new business, becoming a consultant or traveling extensively.

While you may want to spend your first few months in retirement "doing nothing," that desire may soon give way to the urge of becoming productive again. In the surveys conducted on retirement, we found the following goals show up frequently on the soon-to-be retired people's list.

- Mission work
- Consulting in my business field
- Degree/Advanced Degree
- Visit all fifty states
- Write a book
- Foreign travel
- Community work

SPEND TIME NOT MONEY

It's all exciting, but there is a word of caution. Don't let your aggressive pursuit of your goals cause you to spend your retirement savings prematurely. Starting a self-owned business can be great fun in retirement, but don't invest in office construction, equipment and inventory that cannot be returned or resold. One of our clients sold his practice early so he could retire into a start-up business. He was sure that a "group buying company" for the medical profession would be an extremely profitable business. He had spent a large majority of his retirement savings before realizing that he did not have the name, reputation or buying power to compete with the high volume discount sellers. Another client retired early and invested his retirement funds in a company that promised him a managerial position with a chain of clinics. Within two years, the company was in receivership and the doctor had lost nearly all of his retirement savings.

In retirement, time is your cheapest commodity. Use it to your advantage. Before retirement, paying five dollars for a quick car wash between getting off work and picking up the children was worth it. Today, in retirement, you have time. You can turn your time into money whether it's by washing your own car or putting sweat equity (instead of retirement money) into your future projects.

Again, for a vast majority, retirement is not "doing nothing." While it may be okay for a few weeks or even months, most people soon feel the need to accomplish. This is true in part because we have been conditioned over the last forty years to work progressively toward our goals. Our subconscious mind will search for meaning and continue to present us with thoughts and opportunities for advancement.

PSYCHOLOGICAL EFFECTS OF RETIREMENT

Retirement, viewed the wrong way, can be depressing. In fact, depression is common in retirement.

• *We are entering the last one third of our life.* A few generations ago, people only lived two to three years after retirement. Those years were many times associated with failing health. While it's easy to carry on that same mentality from generation to generation, we must realize that the past does not equal the future. Our retirement as a whole will be longer, healthier and more prosperous.

• *Loss of authority.* Many of us spent the last portion of our working life in a position of authority. We had several subordinates working for us and made important decisions on a daily basis. Today, that authority is gone. We have no employees and the company no longer looks to us for direction. This loss of authority can lead to a loss of self-esteem.

• *Loss of respect.* As a working person, we are considered a vital part of society. Once we stop working, many people feel they have lost their ability to contribute to society. While this is not true, even the perception can lead to a loss of self-respect.

• *Loss of routine.* Even routine adds to a sense of self-worth. In our working years, we had to perform certain routines. This routinization gave us direction. In retirement, we must become self-directed to maintain the feeling of accomplishment and satisfaction.

• **Loss of goals.** Working people have goals that are thrust upon them simply because of their work responsibility. In the work place, the show must go on. In other words, many of the working person's goals are there simply because of the job. Retire from your job and you will lose many of your goals. They must be replaced with new goals.

• **Loss of capacity to earn.** For many people, retirement signals a significant decrease in earning capacity. This can easily lead to feelings of inadequacy or loss of security. By pre-planning retirement needs and living according to the plan, those concerns can be lessened.

• **Loss of capacity to catch up.** In our working years, we can ward off, or overcome, almost any financial adversity because we have a work income. In retirement, we become more susceptible to rampant inflation and catastrophic losses, which make us feel more susceptible to the unknown future. With excess time on our hands, we can become preoccupied with the concerns of the unknown future.

RETIREMENT RAMP UP

There is a certain happiness derived from planning pleasant things. Planning a wedding, a vacation or the arrival of a new baby can be exciting. Retirement planning, handled the right way, can be exciting, too. Start by making a list of what you want to do, have, and become, in retirement. Most people can create a list of ten to twenty things they would like to accomplish in retirement. That list will probably take years to accomplish and may well include all the ingredients for a lifetime of happy retirement. The good news is once the list is created, you can start the completion process immediately! Don't make the mistake of waiting to start your retirement activities until you are in your retirement years. By starting those activities now, you will increase your interest and hone your skills for later retirement.

In our retirement focus groups, we found a very sharp division between one group of people who knew exactly what their hobbies would be in retirement and the other group who confessed to having no hobbies or leisure time activities. Those who had no hobbies or leisure time activities knew they wanted and needed some, but had not yet started to develop them. The group with well-defined hobbies and other retirement interests seemed to look forward to retirement and anticipated a happier retirement than those who had not yet considered and cultivated their retirement activities. Defining your mission, writing your goals, and deciding your leisure time activities in advance allows you to retire "into something" as opposed to retiring "into nothing."

Don't sell yourself short. We've all heard the stories of restaurant entrepreneurs, artists and writers who did their greatest works in retirement. In retirement, you will have time freedom. Freedom to be the most creative you have ever been, accomplish your greatest works and perhaps make your biggest contribution to society. Retirement should no longer be viewed as "the sunset years." For many, it will be their most shining moment. Remember, Socrates said, "The unexamined life is not worth living."

13

HEALTH
AND WELLNESS

When you lose your health, you lose your greatest asset in life. Dr. Baldwin had it all. He had retired after selling his practice for over a half million dollars. He had also saved well during his working years. He was active in church, had a great family, and was even making good money in his second career. He exercised regularly and, in fact, completed a marathon just five years ago, days after his 40th birthday.

One afternoon, while bending over to tie his tennis shoes, he felt a slight discomfort in his genital area. He quickly dismissed it as the pains associated with over exercising. But over the next few days, the symptoms increased. Within three weeks, he had symptoms every day, but the symptoms were different than any he had experienced personally or had seen in his years of practice. Some of the symptoms seemed to point to a prostate condition, but it certainly wasn't a textbook case. Before long, every waking minute was consumed by thinking about the symptoms and finding positions and procedures to ease those symptoms, which had now grown to include hypersensitivity in the genital area and a constant dull pain. A visit to his urologist friend ruled out a prostate condition when the digital rectal exam appeared normal and PSA tests (the blood test for prostate infection and/or cancer) came back normal. It seemed that almost overnight a healthy, vibrant, happy individual was transformed into an ailing person controlled by his symptoms and consumed by his search for relief. Additional tests, including a cystoscopy (observation of the inside of the bladder by way of the urethra) and intravenous pyelogram (an x-

ray study of areas of the kidney and urethras) turned up nothing.

Totally perplexed, and at wits end, this doctor decided to bypass other local testing and checked himself in at the Mayo Clinic in Rochester, Minnesota. After an extensive exam and by an internist and neurologist, a series of tests including urine tests, blood tests, an EKG, MRIs, CT Scan, and diagnostic ultrasound were ordered. In the middle of the testing, he was called back for an appointment with the internist who had performed the entrance exam. She informed him that there was no need for the testing to continue. His PSA test results had come back at 11.4! Normal range is 0-4. The diagnosis was narrowed to either a simple prostate infection or prostatic cancer. Because of the doctor's age and his other lab findings, prostate infection was most likely. As a result, he was treated with a heavy dose of antibiotic. But if it was a prostate infection, why wasn't it caught the first time when the PSA test was done locally? Perhaps it was a cancer! The constant stress of the symptoms compounded by a possible cancer diagnosis turned his life into shambles. Everything seemed to be crumbling around him.

Upon returning home, he contacted his urologist, who upon reviewing the records found that his nurse had failed to run a PSA test and had instead mistakenly run a test for HPV. When the test came back, the nurse simply reported to the doctor that all findings were negative. The doctor assumed that included PSA testing. That explained how the prostate condition was missed initially. Now only time would tell if we were looking at a simple prostate infection or prostatic cancer. After four miserable weeks, a new PSA was run. It came back at just 2.4 — well within normal limits. Two months later, a repeat test showed a level of .5. It was simply a prostate infection. The six months struggle from happiness to hell was now over.

It's amazing how plans can be put on hold when you lose your health — your greatest asset in life.

HOW IS YOUR HEALTH?

Few circumstances can hamper your retirement years more than health problems for you or your spouse. Health problems can limit activities, prevent travel and eat up retirement savings. To make matters worse, current retirees appear to be a transitional generation. They, as with previous generations, feel a desire and obligation to help their parents. Their children, on the other hand, may not share that same feeling. The result is that the current retiring generation may very well help their parents, but receive no help in turn from their children. This change is occurring because of both the weakening of the nuclear family and the fact that children and parents tend to live farther apart than in the past. Many of today's retirees will be responsible for their own health and wellness.

THE WELLNESS CONCEPT

We've all seen the cartoon of an old man with the caption that says, "If I had known I was going to live this long, I would have taken better care of my body." While it's meant to be funny, it holds a lot of truth for today's retiree, since the typical retiree today will live fifteen to thirty years in retirement compared two to three years just a few generations ago. We must take better care of our bodies.

The current retiring generation also represents a transitional generation regarding our belief in disease prevention. Past generations waited until they were sick, had a heart attack, or lung cancer to enact the cure. Today, prevention, wellness and maintenance are buzzwords in health care.

Ironically, alternative health care providers, the very ones who were shunned by the medical profession, are the leaders in this movement. Relaxation concepts taught by massage therapists and maintenance care by chiropractors have been an integral part of their treatment plans for years. The resultant effect is a move away from medical care and toward alternative care. The number of visits to medical doctors has dropped 3% since 1990, while visits to alternative health care providers rose over 30% during the same period of time. Today, there are approximately 430 million visits to medical doctors each year compared to 640 million visits to alternative health care providers. In the next decades we will see the use of both medical and alternative health care in the retirees' health maintenance program.

MENTAL HEALTH

Depression is pandemic in older people, but that doesn't mean it is an inevitable part of growing old. Today, we have much more to look forward to in retirement. While retirement gives us lots of time to think, we have the choice in deciding whether to concentrate on the good or the bad. Concentrating on the good, the pure, and the positive naturally creates a healthier outlook.

Self-help psychologists also recommend preparing a "love list" for retirement. This love list is nothing more than a list of things you enjoy doing. Gardening, babysitting grandkids, playing golf, volunteer work, and creative writing make many people's love list. Create your own love list — perhaps fifteen things you love to do. Then simply be sure you do those things on a daily and ongoing basis.

While self-help can certainly brighten your day, it's obvious that chemical changes as we age and external circumstances, like the loss of a loved one, can lead to significant mental stresses that may call for professional help. In the past, our aging citizens were frequently relegated to "second class citizen" status. Certain amounts of depression, disability and illness were accepted as a function of growing older. That may well change now that the demanding baby boomers are hitting retirement. They are not willing to settle for second best or be relegated to "has been" positions. And they shouldn't! They will seek long-term, effective relief from both their mental and physical conditions. "A little bit of depression" will not be okay for the retiree of the future. They should and will continue to work with their health care professionals to maintain optimum mental health.

EXERCISE

If you wear out your body, where are you going to live? People from the past generations spent their working life in hard, physical labor. That, coupled with the lack of medical advancement, caused many people to enter retirement in a "worn out" state. Today retirees are still running, kickboxing and kayaking. Maintaining your physical body will become even more important as you move into retirement. Research shows that diet and exercise can slow aging. As you grow older, changes in your muscles, bones, joints, nerves and blood system will cause a steady decline in strength, reflexes, balance, stamina and flexibility. But there is a lot you can do to slow that deterioration and to maintain a healthy body throughout retirement. Fortunately, we're born with about ten times more physical strength than we need. We have tremendous reserve. And while genetics plays a certain role in your aging process, your diet and exercise can make a big difference as you age. Exercise in retirement should stress cardiovascular and lung endurance, strength, and flexibility.

• *Cardiovascular and Lung Exercise.* Cardiovascular exercise slows the degradation of your heart and blood vessels. Aerobic exercise, such as walking, cycling or running, not only improves heart and lung function, but also wards off depression. Aerobic exercise should be done for at least thirty minutes three times per week. Some work around the home, such as mowing, raking, mopping and vacuuming, may also produce positive cardiovascular effects, but should not be considered a replacement for meaningful exercise.

Retirees can delay the effects of aging if they do age-appropriate exercises. A fifty-year old may still choose to run or cross country cycle and reserve the brisk walks and water aerobics until he is in his 60s or 70s. Granted, as we age, our bones become more brittle, joints develop more wear and we lose some of our range of motion. As a result, we may want to move away from high impact activities, such as running and tennis, and include more low impact activities, such as swimming or stationary cycling.

• *Strengthening.* Muscle mass decreases 40-50% between ages thirty and eighty. This not only means you will lose strength, but it also means you will need to eat less to maintain your weight. (It may also explain why your tapered shirts are starting to fit better upside down!)

Studies in the last decade have found weight training is especially beneficial to older adults. Older people who lift weights an average of three times per week often can double their strength and significantly increase their muscle size and tone in just three months. Lifting weights on consecutive days, however, is not recommended. As the body ages, it takes longer to repair and build muscle. Waiting approximately forty-eight hours between strengthening sessions provides the best results.

• *Flexibility.* Most people forget about improving flexibility during their physical training sessions. But as we grow older, maintaining a flexible body becomes more and more important. As we lose water during the aging process, our connective tissue dries out and becomes less pliable, making our joints stiff. This in turn leads to a greater incident of injury. For instance, as we bend down to touch our toes, the lack of flexibility in the calves and hamstrings may lead to over-stretching of the muscles and other soft tissues in our back, causing low-back injury. The good news is flexibility exercises can be done at almost any time, with very little or no equipment and with or without a partner. Even people with significant health problems should be able to continue their flexibility exercises.

As we grow older, it's important to realize that we do not have to compete with who we were in the past. Your athletic and physical capabilities will naturally decrease with age. If you ran five miles per day in your 30s and 40s, you may be satisfied with three miles per day in your 50s and 60s and a good, brisk, one-mile walk in your 80s.

Studies show that as our arteries grow older, they harden and make it harder for the heart to pump blood through them. As a result, our oxygen consumption capacity declines about 1% per year. So, the same workout will get progressively harder. We also know that there is a continual decline in the number of our motor neurons so muscles won't react as quickly as they did when we were young. And since it's an inevitable part of growing older, we should compensate accordingly so we continue to enjoy our exercise time.

DIET

After all the diets you've heard and read about during the last forty years, the truth is we have probably come full circle in our thinking. A good balanced diet, just as you were taught in grade school, is probably still the best plan. As for nourishing your body as it ages, the best diet is still a moderately low-fat diet with plenty of fruits and vegetables. You should still continue to eat foods from all food groups. Older people do need slightly more protein in that they are not as efficient in using it as they were when they were young. And while the agriculture department's recommendation is about 50-60 grams of protein for people over fifty, many gerentologists suggest 70-90 grams per day.

As we age, we also lose the ability to absorb certain vitamins, minerals and other essential elements. As a result, we will have a continued need for additional vitamins and minerals as supplements to our regular diet. If you listen to all the commercials and read all the printed material, there is no end to the number of vitamins, minerals and other food supplements that you need to take. I once had a patient who, during her initial case history, told me she was taking over ninety vitamin, mineral and other food supplements per day, and, as absurd as that may seem, she was still taking less than one tenth of the supplements available at a well-stocked nutritional outlet! On the other extreme are those senior citizens who suffer repeated bone fractures and never consider supplementing their diets with even the cheapest supplements, such as calcium and vitamin D.

The question then becomes what supplements should we be taking? Even though I had the opportunity to teach nutrition at Palmer Chiropractic College and discussed nutrition with patients during my years in private practice, I have never stumbled upon that perfect formula that's right for everyone. In fact, I'm convinced that there is no "perfect supplement."

Most authorities agree that a good multi-vitamin, especially one formulated for the older person, is a good starting point. You may want to add a good anti-oxidant formula as your second supplement. From then on, your plan will need to be customized. Women who may be at risk for osteoporosis may want to boost their intake of calcium, vitamin D and vitamin B12 to maintain healthy bones and nerve function. Men with a family history of prostate conditions or previous prostate symptoms may want to use Saw Palmetto, and those who suffer from periods of depression may include St. John's Wort or other supplements that show anti-depressive properties.

GOOD HABITS

When we were young, we were invincible — or at least that's what we thought. In fact, alcohol, nicotine and caffeine seemed to give us even more power! But we're not young anymore. Today, a 35-year-old that started smoking as a teenager is on track to cut seventeen years off his life span. A lifetime of borderline excess in alcohol consumption often turns excessive in the years of retirement when faced with so much time and so little responsibility. And the caffeine that acted as a great little pick-me-up now makes us nervous and keeps us awake at night.

Have you ever noticed how certain events — milestones in our life — created the perfect timing to break an old habit? People use these milestones all the time: "I stopped consuming alcohol as soon as I found out I was pregnant...after Jack had his heart attack, we both decided we'd get a little more serious about exercising...when we moved into the new house, I decided it was time to stop smoking."

Retirement provides that same great opportunity. If you are ever going to kick the habit — whatever it is — retirement gives you a great starting point. Since most bad habits come with both a monetary and physical cost, and retirement signals an era of fiscal conservation and concern for wellness, it's a great time to put off old habits and take on a new, healthier lifestyle.

SLEEP

As a child you could sleep through thunderstorms, hurricanes and tornadoes! Now that you're older, a good night's sleep may escape you — and for no apparent good reason. Yet good sleep is paramount to good health and vitality in retirement. In fact, as we age, our bodies again need more sleep to complete the daily repair process.

Sleep authorities suggest there are things you can do to improve your chances of a good night's sleep. First, sleep in total darkness. Partially darkened rooms can give the body the impression of sunset or sunrise and diminish the opportunity for deep sleep. They also suggest creating a routine, that is, going to sleep and waking up at the same time each day improves your chances for restful sleep. Avoiding naps and doing exercises during the day allow the body to function more efficiently during its awake cycle and its sleep cycle.

As a practicing chiropractor, I also have found that most people have been over-sensitized when it comes to choosing a firm mattress. Most people have heard that a firmer mattress is better, but they equate "firm" with "hard." A hard mattress will not increase your ability to sleep well. In fact, as you age, it can create pressure spots on shoulders, hips, knees and elbows that prevent a good night's rest. On the other hand, a firm mattress supports the body well but may have a soft cushion between the support portion of the mattress and your body. This softer, upper support spreads the weight of your body more evenly over the mattress and provides a more restful sleep.

As we age, our body produces less melatonin, a substance frequently associated with sleep. Melatonin can be purchased as a supplement at most health food stores. It has been found to help produce sleep for many older people.

PREVENTION

You are ultimately responsible for your health care. You will decide what health habits to establish, when to see a doctor, and whether you will follow the doctor's advice. You are also responsible for maintaining your prevention and health maintenance programs. You should receive a complete physical each year including blood and urine tests, prostate exams for men, and mammograms and pelvic exams for women. Don't wait for doctors to remind you that it's exam time. You are responsible for scheduling your own maintenance care.

CONDITIONS OF AGING

As we grow older, we become susceptible to different diseases than when we were young. Everyone realizes that there are diseases typically categorized as childhood diseases, diseases of mid-life and diseases of old age. The good news is that as our life span lengthens, new ideas surface to tackle these diseases.

Alzheimer's Disease

Alzheimer's is a degenerative brain disease of unknown cause. It is the most common form of dementia accounting for roughly 60-80% of all dementia in the United States. It usually starts in late middle age or in old age as a memory loss of recent events. Continued memory loss, even for more distant events, progresses over the next five to ten years until there is a profound decline in intelligence to the point of personal helplessness. While there is no cure for Alzheimer's, much progress has been made in the recent years. Drugs are now being tested that seem to significantly delay the progression of Alzheimer's symptoms.

Arthritis

Osteoarthritis is the most common form of arthritis from which four out of five people over age 75 suffer. Mild exercise and joint manipulation appear to retard the progression and reduce symptoms. Medications, such as Celebrex and Vioxx, also appear to reduce the symptoms of this disease. They work much like aspirin but do not irritate the lining of the stomach as aspirin does. Current information also indicates that a combination of glucosamine and chondroitin sulfate may provide some relief from arthritis symptoms.

Another two million Americans suffer from rheumatoid arthritis. This is a more serious inflammation of the joints. It typically attacks the hands, wrists and feet. While rheumatoid arthritis may attack in the teenage years and twenties, it is seen most frequently after age fifty.

Cancer

The bad news: Over 500,000 people die from cancer each year. The good news: An estimated 8.2 million people are alive today following the diagnosis of cancer. Many people feel that we are on the verge of widespread cancer prevention. As mentioned earlier, routine annual exams can help with early detection, the best indicator of recovery.

Cataracts

Cataracts are a clouding of the lens of the eye or its surrounding transparent membrane. That clouding obstructs the passage of light, making it difficult to see clearly or discern colors. The good news is an estimated 2.3 million cataract surgeries are performed each year and in most cases are very successful.

Congestive Heart Failure

Currently, nearly five million people are living with congestive heart failure. Another 400,000 new cases are diagnosed each year. Congestive heart failure affects people of all ages but is more common in senior citizens. The good news is while congestive heart failure is progressive, managed correctly, it can still provide many years of normal living. Recently, two pacemaker-like devices have reached the final stages of testing and could be on the market shortly. While the implants may not prolong life, they can keep the heart beating in sync, enabling patients to have a better quality of life.

Hearing Loss

Thirty million Americans suffer some type of hearing loss, but only six million use hearing aids. The same digital technology that improves computers and televisions also provides vast improvements for hearing aid devices. One company has recently introduced a $39 disposable hearing aid that delivers superb quality, but only lasts for forty days. Perhaps hearing aids will become disposable much like contact lenses.

Depression

Depression is a common and highly treatable disorder. Most people who suffer depression can return to pre-depression levels with proper care. Today, it's no longer considered normal for senior citizens to have a "certain level of depression." Psychological and psychiatric help provide relief to a vast majority of people who seek help.

Diabetes

Diabetes, while it affects people of all ages, develops more commonly in later life and tends to run in families. Nearly sixteen million people (or 6% of the population in the United States) have diabetes. Each day, approximately 2,200 people are diagnosed with diabetes. Symptoms include thirst, weight loss and fatigue. Most cases of diabetes can be managed: some by diet and others by insulin injection. Some insulin-dependent diabetics now use a "pump," which constantly delivers measured amounts of insulin to the body. Researchers are also working on oral insulin and have had recent success in transplanting the human tissue, which allows diabetics to produce insulin on their own.

Failing Eyesight

The most serious age-related eyesight condition is macular degeneration. It is the leading cause of blindness in people over fifty. Visudyne, a new drug, shows good promise for reducing or stopping macular degeneration.

Farsightedness, which usually develops in the forties, appears to respond well to laser surgery — similar to the method used to correct nearsightedness. This new surgery for farsightedness is now in the final stages for being approved for use nationwide.

Glaucoma

Glaucoma actually refers to a group of diseases that have common features including pressure inside the eye, damage to the optic nerve, and visual field loss. There are usually no symptoms and no warning signs, so early diagnosis and treatment are the keys to managing the diseases.

Heart Attack

A heart attack, or myocardial infarction, occurs when one of the blood vessels that supplies oxygen to the heart becomes blocked. The area of the heart that does not receive blood begins to die. The seriousness of a heart attack depends on how much a heart is affected. Often the surrounding healthy muscle keeps working, allowing the heart to keep pumping while the injured muscle heals and recovers some of its strength. Monitoring your blood pressure, exercising and medication when needed, greatly reduce the risk associated with heart attack. Recent studies have also shown that an aspirin a day may reduce the seriousness of heart attack.

Menopause

About one third of the women in the United States today, more than thirty-six million, have been through menopause. With a life expectancy of over eighty years, a fifty-year-old woman can expect to live more than one third of her life after menopause. For some women, menopause is nearly symptomless. For others, symptoms include sweats, nervousness, and irritability. Today, however, the symptoms that were almost expected a generation or two ago can now be alleviated or totally eliminated through the use of various supplements, herbs and medications.

Osteoporosis

Osteoporosis is a weakening of the bones that affects 28 million older Americans. It is much more common in women. Bone density testing, which is now available for less than $100, can assess bone mineral density (BMD) and your chance of developing osteoporosis. Osteoporosis can lead to hip fractures, spinal fractures and general bone deformation. Increases in calcium and vitamin D along with products that increase absorption will decrease the chances of suffering hip fractures or other bone disease. In severe cases, estrogen replacement may be needed. Estrogen replacement can, however, increase the risk of breast cancer. Recently, alternative drugs, such as Raloxifene, are being used to mimic estrogen's effects without the danger of increasing breast cancer risk.

Periodontal Disease

Periodontal disease is any disease affecting the supporting structures of the teeth. As we age, we may experience bone recession from around the roots of the teeth. Both non-surgical and surgical periodontal therapies can control most forms of periodontal disease.

Sexual Dysfunction

Sexual dysfunction is a generic term that includes female orgasmic disorder and sexual arousal disorder in females and erectile dysfunction and male orgasmic disorder in men. By now, everyone has heard of Viagra and other drugs and devices used to improve sexual function. Married couples without sexual dysfunction can expect to continue sexual activity into their 80s. Today, many sexual dysfunctions can be eliminated or managed through proper health care. Senior citizens should not allow sexual dysfunction to reduce their happiness in retirement.

Urinary Incontinence

Some seventeen million Americans suffer from weak bladder control. Eighty-five percent of those people are women. As we grow older, the problem increases. Fifty percent of the nursing home population suffers from incontinence. Pelvic exercises are the most common treatment for urinary incontinence. Alternative health care providers, such as chiropractors, provide information, advice and relief for some types of urinary incontinence, and many people feel that certain supplements reduce the risk of urinary incontinence. Some drugs and minimally invasive surgeries are now also being used.

The greatest factor in predicting your health in retirement is you. A healthy lifestyle, periodic exams, preventive health care, and a positive mental attitude can greatly increase the potential for healthy retirement years. Treat your body with kindness and respect and you can expect many healthy, happy years in retirement.

14
YOUR HOBBIES

Everyone has a favorite little restaurant. A husband and wife who are semi-retired own mine. Normally half the fun of eating there is the spirited conversation of the couple, but one night when we stopped in for dinner, things were a little different. The husband seemed very abrupt — almost withdrawn. After a brief conversation, he disappeared into the kitchen.

"What's wrong with Don?" I asked his wife as she stepped up to take the order. "Aw, he's bent out of shape because he lost about $500,000 in the stock market this week and he has to cash it in," she replied in a somewhat unsympathetic tone. "He invests in some high-risk stock, loses it all, and then mopes around all day."

What a tragedy — a retiree losing a majority of his retirement savings — and how could his wife show no concern? "I'm really sorry to hear that," I said. To which she responded, "Aw, it doesn't really make any difference, it's just play money."

"What do you mean?" I asked. And with a wave of her hand as if to say, "oh it isn't anything," she said, "He plays this stupid fantasy stock market game with his friends. He wasn't doing as well as some of them, so he invested in some long shots. This weekend they meet together to decide how everybody ranked, and right now, I'd guess he's on the bottom. The way he acts, you'd think it was real money."

Everybody needs a hobby — even if it's occasionally frustrating. Your interest in your hobbies and use of leisure time will, to a large extent, dictate your happiness in retirement.

IT'S TIME TO PLAY

As a retired person, you will have more leisure time than ever before. You can use your time however you wish. You can sleep late, stay up late — or both! In one sense, time seems to speed up as we get older. In another sense, it slows down. Activities like grocery shopping used to be something sandwiched between getting off work and attending parent-teacher conferences. Now, it's a whole day event.

Hobbies will help you create your own private utopia. You should discover before you leave full-time work what your passions are and explore how you will pursue them once you retire. Then, based on your assessment of the satisfaction those activities will give you, build a retirement agenda.

TRAVEL

Travel is by far the most popular leisure activity during the early years of retirement. Some retirees explore all the places they have dreamed about during the last fifty years. Others return to the same vacation spot year after year, combining the excitement of travel with the comfort of returning to a familiar location. Traveling is a way to see new sights, meet new people, learn new things and explore your yet unknown.

Being a senior citizen can make traveling less expensive. Most travel-related businesses provide senior citizen discounts either through membership discounts such as AARP or directly. Many airlines offer special programs for senior citizens — usually 10% off all airfares.

When traveling there are many ways to save. Make use of every senior citizen advantage.

• For cruises and other travel activities that are usually booked to capacity, reserving early can provide the best discount. In other cases, waiting until the last minute and being flexible will provide discounts.

• Shopping the Internet can provide great last minute deals if you have the flexibility to travel with short notice.

• Mention your age when making traveling plans. Travel agents and other businesses may not be aware of your age unless you inform them. Sometimes you must be even more specific and ask for the highest discount provided senior citizens.

• Some travel activities and locations are especially senior citizen friendly. Over half of all the passengers on cruise ships are over fifty. In fact, some ships cater almost exclusively to the retirement crowd. Sometimes whole communities are retirement friendly, offering senior discounts and senior related activities as the norm.

SPORTS AND RECREATION

In the early '60s, John F. Kennedy brought America's "physical condition" to the public's attention. He encouraged regular physical exercise for the youth. That was forty years ago and the effects on the retirement generation are still being seen. Retirees are participating in various levels of physical activity — much more than our fathers and mothers did. Today, it's common to see a 55-year-old on his daily run. One generation ago, if a 55-year-old was seen running, we assumed someone must be chasing him! How many miles per week did your father or mother run while in their 50s and 60s? We are indeed the generation of active retirees.

To be able to retire "into" an active hobby, you need to start that hobby in your pre-retirement years. Our focus groups showed that there were two distinct groups entering retirement — those with defined hobbies that they already enjoy and plan on continuing in retirement, and others who had no idea of what they will be doing with their leisure time in retirement.

If your hobbies include sports and recreation, they provide a double benefit. First, they provide a pleasant way to spend leisure time, and second, they promote good health. If your future leisure activities include activities to provide physical conditioning, it's important to choose the right activities for your age and present state of health. As we said earlier, retirees in their 50s and 60s may still be running and even competing in races. For them, brisk walking will be reserved for their 70s and 80s! Be sure you choose a physical activity commensurate with your age and physical health.

PICKING THE RIGHT ACTIVITY

Factors other than physical ability must also be considered. Is the equipment expensive? Does your activity require the use of a public field or course? Do you need other players? Can you play year-round? Are there dues, memberships and other costs that may become prohibitive over time? Is the activity satisfying?

Recently, a golfer told me a story that he reports to be true. His golf party of four was following a golfer who was having an extremely frustrating day. Following yet another bad drive, the golfer picked up his clubs — bag and all — and threw them into the lake, got in his cart and drove off. Amazed, the party behind him continued to play through, planning to retrieve the bag and clubs after they had completed the hole. But, before they had the opportunity, the golfer returned in his golf cart, stopped by the lake, took off his shoes and socks, rolled up his pant legs, and waded into the water. Then he picked up his golf bag, unzipped the pocket, retrieved his car keys, zipped the bag shut, threw it back into the lake and drove off. Apparently, the man's hobby was not as satisfying as he might have hoped!

The most common physical activities in retirement include:

• *Golf.* Many men and women dream about retirement and the opportunity to golf nearly every day. The advantages of golf are that you can continue it as an activity into late retirement and it provides social as well as physical activity. In fact, golf can provide the perfect link between the 65-year-old retiree and the 35-year-old up-and-coming business entrepreneur — his son. Golf, however, considering the cost of the equipment, club memberships and course fees, can be costly. It frequently calls for pre-planning and can be seasonal depending on the climate of the area.

• **Walking**. Almost everyone can participate in walking. It's low cost, easily accomplished and can be done by yourself or with friends. Some retirees avoid the seasonal effects by walking in enclosed malls and shopping centers during inclement weather. It's also a great activity to carry into later retirement.

• **Fishing**. Fishing is a great pastime for many retirees. It can provide social interaction or time alone — in solitude. We've all heard the story of the retiree who cast a bare hook into the water. When asked why he didn't use a worm, he responded that he was afraid that if he used a worm, he would catch a fish! Though fishing qualifies as a sport, it may not provide the same level of physical activity as other sports, but can be carried into later retirement.

• **Running**. Running is usually reserved for early retirement years, though people have been known to run — and in fact compete — into their late 80s and 90s. Since running is low cost and does not require special courses or memberships, it's an excellent activity for the retiree who is still on the go. Because running is a high-impact sport, it must be tempered with sufficient resting time to rebuild tissue.

• **Aerobics**. Aerobic training is a great activity for retirees in that the physical demand can range from high impact aerobic exercise, such as kickboxing, to low-impact, low-intensity aerobics, like water aerobics. Aerobic activities can be done in a group setting or individually. Today, there are all types of aerobics classes — Jazzercise, Dancercise, Believercise (aerobic exercise to Christian music), and about any other "cise" you want.

• **Tennis.** Tennis provides great physical activity for the young retiree but may be seasonal or costly depending on memberships and court fees. Tennis may also create more injuries for the aging athlete. Sudden stops and starts can affect feet, ankles, knees, hips and lower back. Serving and overhead drives frequently affect the shoulder, and racquet vibration can cause tennis elbow.

• **Weight lifting.** Weight lifting is rapidly increasing in popularity among retirees. In addition to providing physical fitness, it also improves the strength and appearance of the body. It can be done in a gym or at home with friends or by yourself. And studies show that weight lifting as well as other weight-bearing activities improves bone strength.

• **Swimming.** Swimming is one of the most complete physical activities available. It improves cardiovascular function, range of motion and muscle tone. It is low impact and can be adjusted according to physical ability and age. These values must be weighed against the disadvantages of access to a pool, climate (in the case of outdoor swimming) and other conditions that may be associated with prolonged contact with the water.

• **Boating.** For some people, the perfect picture of retirement is sailing into the sunset on a boat. Boating, though expensive, can be fun. The amount of physical activity can vary from rigorous sailing to relaxed shoreline cruises. Boating usually involves more activity than simply getting in a boat and riding through the water. Docking, trailering, and watercraft upkeep also provide physical activity.

SPORTS AND FITNESS TIPS

If you are not currently involved in a sport or physical fitness activity, you may want to consider the following:

• Many sporting activities have master's clubs and functions for older athletes.

• If you decide to participate in a sporting activity, do it with enough frequency to avoid injury and maintain enough skill to participate on the same level as other team players.

• You may enjoy your physical activities more if you do not feel the urge to compete. Though I still continue to run in distance races, I long ago quit counting my position.

• If you are not already involved in a physical activity, you may find that your willingness to "stay with" the activity is predicated on how much work it takes to become involved in the activity. If you have to call ahead for reservations, line up a playing partner, collect your equipment and drive to a club or field, you may be tempted to forgo any physical activity that day. Make your ability to exercise as easy and pleasant as possible.

• Activities that are done in a group can create a better social life but may have limits as to when they are available. For instance, you can only bowl with your bowling league during scheduled times. As a result, it's best to have more than one physical activity, some that can be done individually and some in a group.

EDUCATION AS A HOBBY

I fully intend to complete another degree sometime in retirement. A college near our home offers a Master's Degree in Business that sounds quite appealing. Others may want to take just a class or two. One retiree recently bragged that since taking a small engine repair class at his community college more than five years ago, he has never found a small engine that he could not repair. His continued education has provided him with a hobby *and* a source of income.

You, too, may want to spend some of your leisure time taking different courses or even getting a graduate or post-graduate degree. Retirement gives you the time to pursue knowledge — now in the areas that are interesting to you as opposed to areas required by your work or for the completion of a degree. Schools now offer courses for retirees on subjects ranging from small engine repair to computer programming.

Colleges are also starting to provide classes for the "atypical" student. Colleges — both community colleges and four-year colleges — are providing opportunities to take courses at local high schools. Many colleges provide significant discounts or even free classes to people over 60. For a listing of the colleges in your area that offer free or discounted tuition, write the Institute of Lifetime Learning, AARP, 1909 K Street, N.W., Washington, D.C., 20049.

Here's another twist to participating in the classroom. Instead of being a student, why not become a teacher? You may be surprised at what you have in terms of knowledge and skills that could be taught in a classroom setting. Not all classrooms are college classrooms. Churches, retirement centers, private schools, businesses, daycare centers and seminar settings provide lots of opportunities to teach.

My grandfather took the opportunity to teach Sunday school and Bible study in the retirement home he lived in until age 92. Perhaps it's time to share your knowledge.

OTHER NON-SPORT HOBBIES

There are perhaps as many potential hobbies as there are retirees in the nation. Here's a short list of the hobbies of the soon-to-be retirees in our focus groups:

- Raising turtles
- Political activist
- Catering parties
- Teaching children's dance
- Ham radio activities

- Gideon activities (a Christian service organization)
- Engine maintenance and repair
- Fishing
- Quilting
- Woodworking
- Consulting
- Playwriting
- Public speaking
- Telephone prayer line
- Singing

Some of these hobbies may sound interesting to you, others may sound very boring simply because you have no interest in them. One way to increase your interest in your own hobby is to find others with the same interests. It's almost like finding a support group — for your hobby.

Don't limit yourself to one hobby. Spreading your time over two or three hobbies allows a change of pace and helps fill a void in the event you reach a point where you cannot continue one of your hobbies. Running is a great hobby and provides physical exercise, but what will you do if an injury prevents you from continuing?

HOBBIES THAT PRODUCE INCOME

Some of us were fortunate enough to have our hobby become our lifetime profession. Others may find that opportunity only in retirement. Often people work part time in retirement as a consultant to their previous profession. Consulting is a hobby to them. Others choose a totally unrelated hobby and turn it into a business. One retiree, who taught all his life, found that his summer job, house painting, became a great hobby. He found he could work as little or as much as he wanted, bid only the easy jobs that called for no climbing, and that it provided good income. Another retiree found her interest in arts and crafts translated well into a second business of assembling gift baskets, which she sells to businesses who give them as gifts to their valued customers.

Again, one word of caution; don't become over-optimistic in your prospects for converting your hobby to a profitable business. While the investment of time is a good idea, the investment of retirement savings should be done with extreme caution.

HOBBIES IN LATER RETIREMENT

Will your current hobbies serve you well in your later retirement years — or will they be too physically demanding? Can you continue them if your life becomes more sedentary? Again, it's a great idea to have more than one hobby — and some that can be carried into later retirement. There are lots of opportunities. Your generation will be the first to use the Internet in retirement for pleasure and profit. Writing — poems, short stories, family histories and even novels — can continue into later retirement years. Voice recognition software now makes even the most limited typist prolific. Others prefer to be on the other end of the book and become quite interested in reading. Arts and crafts including painting, carving, woodworking and needlepoint can also be continued into later retirement.

For many retired people, their hobbies are their life. Their hobbies consume their time, provide their social life and give satisfaction that was not available during their working years. Others never seem to find the right hobbies and the satisfaction that accompanies them. Hobbies can greatly increase your happiness in retirement. Choose them early and carefully.

15

INSURANCE

I t was 7:30 a.m. on a hot Saturday morning. Later in the day, the temperature would top out at 106 degrees and the heat index at 112 degrees. My wife, my daughter and I had signed up for the Thunder Run, a two-mile fun run sponsored by the Army National Guard. We started toward the back of the pack, but soon overtook an older gentleman running at a somewhat measured pace. After about ¾ of a mile, my wife and I decided to walk. Before long, our older friend overtook us and built a 20-yard lead. Now, it was time for us to run again. We soon passed him and a few others. Just past the mile point, we walked again — and he passed us. As we turned the corner, we had the wind behind us and a downhill stretch. We again ran and again passed him. But as we turned into the wind for the last half-mile, we decided walking was more fun! The older runner passed us by forty yards. Less than 200 yards from the finish, my wife and I started to run again. We passed under the clock two steps behind the man who ran with a slow, steady pace. They announced the finishers over the loudspeakers, "George Rejda finishes, and David and Linda Kats make it back, too." How embarrassing — we had reached the age when we were being complimented for "making it back." The most interesting thing I heard, however, was that George Rejda had finished just in front of us. George was an icon in the business department at the University of Nebraska. I took Econ 107 — Insurance — from him in 1967.

As we left the finish area and made our way back to the car I noticed Dr. Rejda just a few steps behind us. I dropped back with his group and confirmed that he used to teach at the University of Nebraska. "Yes, in fact I still do —

I teach insurance," he replied. I shared with him that I had taken his class and felt it was the most informative and interesting class of my undergraduate studies.

1967 — that was the Vietnam era — attendance was required at all the university classes. We sat alphabetically. I was seat 107 — between Isley and Kirkland. I learned an enormous amount in that class. Where else can you learn about insurance from someone who isn't selling it!

As we headed back to the car, we talked about his teaching style — using stories to illustrate a concept. It filled his class year after year even though many students were taking it as an elective. I reminded him of my favorite story. He was illustrating the concept of "narrow interpretation" of insurance terms. In his illustration, the term was "double indemnity" (where the insurance company pays double the amount of insurance if the death was accidental). He said that for someone to die an accidental death, it had to be by "violent and external means." His story was of a man who had consumed too much alcohol, left the drinking establishment, slipped off a curb, hit his head, was knocked unconscious and eventually died. Autopsy found, however, that before he died, he had vomited and aspirated his own vomit! The insurance company refused to pay because while the death was violent, they ruled that because of the asphyxiation of vomit, the death was not by external means. Wow! What a story to remember.

As we parted, I thanked him again. Walking away, I realized that the information he had given me had saved/made me at least an extra $100,000 over my lifetime.

We got home and showered — it was still before ten, which was good news because today was the day I had decided to start writing chapter fifteen of Going Out On Top — Insurance.

INSURANCE

Other than my experience with Dr. Rejda, I hate insurance! Someone once said that paying alimony was like feeding oats to a dead horse. To me, paying insurance premiums ranks right up there in the same category. I pay life insurance premiums, health insurance premiums, disability insurance premiums, malpractice insurance premiums, and liability insurance premiums — and I never collect...but then considering what I'd have to do to collect, I guess I shouldn't complain!

In this chapter, we'll cover just the basics of insurance in an easy-to-understand format. In retirement, you'll probably have need for five major types of insurance:

1. Life Insurance
2. Health Insurance
3. Medicare/MediGap Insurance
4. Long-term Care Insurance
5. Property and Liability Insurance

The good news is: As you reach retirement your need for some types of insurance goes away. For doctors and lots of other health care professionals the need to purchase malpractice insurance goes away, assuming you have adequate tail coverage and you're sure you will no longer be treating patients — even on a voluntary basis. If you do continue to practice, malpractice insurance for the part-time practitioner can be very inexpensive. Disability insurance to protect your earned income stream can also be dropped at or even before retirement. While disability insurance is important in mid-life, when you reach retirement, you no longer have a stream of earned income to protect. So the closer you get to retirement, the less valuable disability insurance becomes.

MAKING THE MOST OF YOUR INSURANCE

Insurance can give great peace of mind, but today insurance companies offer such a wide variety of policies that it's difficult to determine which policies are necessary and which policies are best for you. First, remember the primary reason for insurance is to guard against the loss from catastrophic occurrences. This basic premise should keep you from buying unnecessary insurance or becoming over-insured. Generally speaking, small losses can be replaced without the use of insurance. In other words, never insure for ordinary losses. This same concept suggests that you should take advantage of high deductibles whenever possible. Obviously, the term "high deductible" has different meanings for different people. A high-income family may be able to purchase health insurance with a $2,000 or even $5,000 deductible. To them, the possibility of having to pay $3,000 or $4,000 out of pocket for health care is feasible. Other families cannot afford this risk.

Throughout your life, you must also manage your insurance. Your needs for health insurance, life insurance and other types of insurance will vary according to your age, profession and risk level. Avoid being over-insured (buying every policy presented to you) or having overlapping policies.

INSURANCE AGENTS

There is more to managing your insurance correctly than simply buying the right policy. The administration of those policies is also important — that's where the human factor comes in. Many insurance agents have had advanced training in insurance, financial planning, estate planning and other similar fields, and have CLU, ChFC, LUTCF or similar designations behind their name. This extra training can be valuable to you. Find insurance agents that you enjoy working with and who have your best interests at heart. Work with an agent who is as willing to help you file a claim as sell a policy. Don't be afraid to switch insurance agents if you are unsatisfied, but realize that it is also important to maintain a certain "history" with the professionals who will help you throughout retirement. This may mean that as you grow older, you begin to work with professionals who are younger than you — therefore, gaining the advantage of not having to switch professionals in later life. In the last ten years, I have switched dentists from a grandfather to his grandson, switched asset protection professionals from a father who is older than me to a son who is younger, switched attorneys from someone older than me to his son, and chosen a new medical doctor and insurance agent who are younger than I am. In each case, the transition from the older professional to the younger was done over a period of time and with the blessing of the older professional. While switching to professionals who are younger than you is no guarantee that they will continue to service you (I retired from active chiropractic practice at age thirty-eight), it certainly increases your odds.

DISABILITY INSURANCE

If you will still be working several years before retiring, you may consider disability insurance. Disability insurance allows you to protect your retirement savings in the event of unexpected disability. The cost and benefits of disability policies vary greatly. That's due in part because the definition of disability varies from policy to policy. Some disability policies pay if you are not able to continue in your profession. Others pay if you are unable to continue in your profession or a related profession. For instance, a surgeon who suffers the loss of his hand may not be able to continue with surgery, but can work in a related field, such as teaching in a medical school. Whether he receives disability is determined by his policy's definition of "disabled."

The best way to save on disability insurance is to increase the elimination period — the period before benefits are available. Some physicians feel they will continue to receive income from their practice (by collecting accounts receivable) during the first few months of disability. As a result, they have a longer waiting period before receiving benefits.

The amount of disability insurance you purchase will also help determine the premium amount. Normally, people purchase disability insurance to cover approximately 60% of their salary. Your income will also determine the maximum amount of disability insurance you are qualified to purchase. A person with a monthly salary of $5,000 will not be allowed to buy a $10,000 disability policy.

The premium amount will also vary based on the length of time the insurance company continues to pay disability. Many plans automatically stop covering you when you reach age sixty-five. If you have adequate retirement savings and are nearing retirement, you may consider dropping your disability insurance.

It is also important to choose whether to pay the disability insurance premium personally (making the claim benefits tax free when received) or to have your business pay the premiums as a tax deductible business expense (which makes the benefits taxable as income when received).

There is, however, a hybrid strategy if you operate as a corporation and have a medical and disability reimbursement plan. You pay the premiums personally throughout the year and at year's end when you already know that there will be no claims, you have the corporation reimburse you. You can then start the cycle over the following year. This is an aggressive strategy which has passed the IRS test as legal.

LIFE INSURANCE

The reasons for life having insurance change as you age. In your younger and middle years, the major reason for life insurance is to protect your family in the event of your premature death — to give them income to live on when they are without your income. It will allow them to remain in the same house, finance college education and readjust to a lifestyle that they will have without you and your income. In later life, assuming you have saved adequately for retirement, insurance provides liquidity for the estate. Your life insurance can be placed in an Irrevocable Trust and used to cover estate taxes, probate fees, legal fees, inheritance tax, and if you are a business owner, to keep your business in operation until it can be taken over or disposed of properly.

If you do not have a large estate, you may even want to drop your life insurance policy. But, if your insurance policy is other than a term policy, you have some other options.

• *You can cash in your policy.* If you're a good investor, you may very well be able to get a better return on your money than by allowing the insurance company to invest the money — but remember, you will be taxed on any gain.

• *Take a paid-up policy.* A paid-up policy can be a very good idea. Basically, you inform the insurance company that you will no longer be paying premiums and, in exchange, they reduce the amount of your policy — but it still stays in effect.

• *Convert to an annuity.* Instead of taking the cash from your policy, you can receive an annuity — a monthly income for life. Once you turn sixty-five, insurance agents realize that there's very little need for you to purchase more insurance. As a result, they may concentrate their efforts on getting you to convert your present policies into annuities. If you do convert to an annuity, be sure it is a section 1035 exchange. And because of the wide variation in payouts, you will need to shop around for the best deal.

TERM VS. WHOLE LIFE

Term insurance is "pure" insurance. You pay an insurance premium and receive only insurance. Whole life insurance, on the other hand, is a life insurance policy with an attached savings account.

Term Insurance

You can buy the same amount of term insurance much cheaper than whole life insurance. People who feel they need life insurance but cannot afford the premiums should certainly consider term insurance. As the name implies, term insurance is life insurance for a specific term — a number of years. The term typically ranges from one to twenty years. Term insurance is usually not available after seventy-five years old, so you may find yourself paying for term insurance for many years on which your estate will never collect.

There are three major types of term insurance: annual renewable term, level term, and decreasing term. Annual renewable term, as the name implies, allows you to renew the same amount of insurance on an annual basis for a specified number of years. Because the chances of death increase as you age, the premium goes up to allow the policy to keep the same limits. Level term or straight term works much the same way, except that you pay the same premium over the term of the contract by over paying in early years and under paying in later years. Decreasing term allows you to pay the same premium over the life of the contract but compensates for the increased risk by decreasing the amount paid upon death.

Term insurance is an excellent life insurance choice for people who may need insurance for only a few years, such as when selling or purchasing a business where you are a key figure. It's also perfect for those who need life insurance and cannot afford higher premiums, as well as for people who are disciplined and experienced investors and feel that they can beat the return on investment offered by whole life insurance.

Whole Life Insurance

Whole life insurance is both an insurance plan and a savings plan. As a result, you buy far less insurance coverage for each premium dollar when compared to term insurance. On the other hand, whole life and other similar ordinary life insurance policies provide many people with a "forced" savings plan.

Whole life insurance was very popular four or five decades ago. Social Security was somewhat new, and the low inflation rate of the time made the insurance companies' 4-6% return on investment look good. Once inflation increased, investment counselors started to proliferate and competition from financial institutions increased, whole life insurance quickly fell into disfavor. Investment strategists convinced the public that they would be much better off buying cheaper term insurance and investing the remainder of their premium dollar on their own. They were probably right — making one major assumption — that the person buying the term insurance would actually invest the remainder of the money that was previously spent on premiums. Unfortunately, many people simply dropped their whole life insurance, cashed it in or took a paid-up policy and then bought term insurance, but they never used the difference saved in premiums as investment capital. As a result, today, we see people who have a false security. They feel they have life insurance. Many of these insured will become uninsurable as they grow older and reach the end of their term life insurance contract unless they are willing to pay substantially for higher premiums. This means that they will have no savings and no life insurance.

Somewhat in response to whole life insurance falling into disfavor, new forms of whole life, or ordinary life insurance, were developed, such as universal life insurance. By and large, these new "insurance plus savings" policies do provide a better ROI than the old whole life policies.

OTHER INSURANCE CONCEPTS

Some things I just don't understand. When I was a young boy, the proper amount to tip at a restaurant was 10%. By the time I reached middle age, it was 15%. Now, it's pushing 20%. If the cost of a meal has gone up with inflation over the years, wouldn't a 10% gratuity be as adequate today as it was forty years ago? The same thing is true of life insurance needs. When I was young, the rule of thumb said you should have life insurance equivalent to five times your annual salary. Today, books suggest you should have insurance equal to seven to ten times your annual salary. What's changed? Now, I realize some things have changed. An increased inflation rate, for instance, makes money worth less over time, and of course, your spouse (the assumed beneficiary) has a longer life expectancy in retirement than previous generations had. But in the case of life insurance, the general rule of thumb is probably too general to be of value. While some people may indeed need ten times their annual salary, other people need no life insurance at all. How much insurance would you suggest Bill Gates and Warren Buffet need?

As discussed earlier, while ordinary life insurance may not provide the highest return on investment, it does provide a forced savings plan throughout your life. If you are not a good saver, some type of "insurance plus savings" life insurance may have value to you. Another value of these forced savings is that the savings accumulate tax deferred and can be placed in an Irrevocable Trust where they may be able to be distributed to your heirs estate-tax free.

It is important to purchase life insurance from a reputable company in that you will be relying on them to hold your savings for perhaps your entire life. The stability of your life insurance company is very important to your estate.

If you're already retired or will be retiring in the next few years, you're probably best avoiding an expensive insurance policy completely.

HEALTH INSURANCE

One of the disadvantages of early retirement is the potential loss of your company's health insurance benefits. Where are you going to get health insurance for you and your family between your retirement and age sixty-five? In many cases, it's best to keep your employer-provided health insurance. Health insurance costs have skyrocketed over the past years. In 1995, the average sixty-two-year old paid nearly $5,000 per year in health care. By 2000, that cost rose to $7,500.

Employer-provided health insurance is probably your best health insurance option before you are Medicare eligible. This is especially true if your employer picks up a portion of your health care costs in retirement. Even without the employer's contribution, continuing your previous health care coverage is probably best in that 1) it's usually cheaper than purchasing private health insurance, 2) you're already covered and can avoid policy lapses and new physical exams, and 3) you know the coverage and are familiar with the policy.

Unfortunately, increasingly high insurance costs are causing many employers to cut back on insurance coverage, and one of the best places to trim the budget is by dropping health coverage for former employees. According to a National Center for Health Services research report, 49% of retired people fifty-five years or older have some form of health insurance through their former employer.

If your former employer does provide a portion or all of your health care coverage in retirement, be sure to see that your coverage remains the same in retirement. The company may limit your coverage or the coverage of dependents once you reach retirement. Your spouse could also be included in certain limitations. And if insurance rates go up, the insurance company may pass that increase on to you.

COBRA

The Consolidated Omnibus Budget Reconciliation Act of 1985 (COBRA) states that all companies with twenty or more employees must allow former employees to continue buying the company's group health policy if they retire from the company prior to age sixty-five. According to COBRA, the company must provide health insurance coverage for no less than eighteen months and at no more than 102% of the premium the company would pay. While this may seem expensive, it will probably still be cheaper than individual health insurance. Even after your COBRA coverage ends, you will likely be able to convert your employer's group policy into a personal insurance policy without the need to demonstrate insurability. Once you reach Medicare age, the company's obligation is terminated.

Medicare

Medicare began providing benefits to nineteen million seniors on July 1, 1966. Now, more than thirty-nine million seniors and disabled citizens have coverage. And according to American Medical News, Medicare enrollment is expected to reach seventy-seven million in 2030. "Medicare is one of the most popular federal programs and universally gets high marks from beneficiaries and members of their family," according to Donna Shalala, Ph.D., Secretary of the Department of Health and Human Services.

There are two parts to Medicare — appropriately named Part A and Part B. While you must sign up for Medicare to be eligible, Part A, which covers hospital costs, is free to all people age sixty-five (except for a few who may have less than ten years of work credits). Medicare Part B covers doctor services, outpatient hospital services, durable medical equipment such as wheel chairs and in-home oxygen equipment, and other supplies not covered by Part A. You are automatically enrolled in Part B when you sign up for Part A. If you do not want to enroll in Part B, you must elect not to take it. Part B premiums can be automatically deducted from the enrollee's Social Security benefits.

Continued adequate funding of Medicare seems likely in that politicians are now considering placing Medicare surpluses in a lock box. This Medicare lock box would ensure that the funds for Medicare Part A could be spent only on the Medicare Part A program. The lock box concept, however, would do nothing to protect Medicare Part B that pays for private physicians and other professional services. Most people, however, are not concerned about Medicare Part B running out of money since it is financed, at least in part, by the monthly premiums paid by Medicare enrollees.

Because of the free coverage in Part A and the reasonable premiums for Part B, Medicare covers the vast majority of the nation's health care costs for people sixty-five and older. Medicare, however, does not cover all health care expenses. First, its coverage is closely aligned with the typical medical model — paying well for treatment of disease, but paying little attention to preventive care. And in keeping with the medical model of care, it also reduces payment or does not cover care provided by non-MD health care providers. For example, eyeglasses and hearing aids — greatly needed by senior citizens — are not covered by Medicare. Chiropractic coverage by Medicare is also severely restricted and many other types of alternative health care are not covered at all.

Perhaps the biggest shortfall of Medicare is its lack of coverage for prescription drugs. Congress is currently working on legislation that would provide coverage.

MediGap Insurance

Because Medicare does not cover *all* health care costs of the enrollee, 75% of the people covered by Medicare also have private health insurance called MediGap insurance. MediGap insurance is used to pick up the difference between what Medicare pays and the actual cost of the care. MediGap policies used to vary greatly, but today, federal law requires that insurers offer no more than ten standard MediGap policies. Each policy must provide the core benefits. A policy with only the core benefits is designated "Plan A." Each of the successive plans — plans B through J — adds more benefits to the core. All insurance companies that offer MediGap plans must offer the core policy. Beyond that, they can offer any of the other extended policies they want.

With a few exceptions, everyone eligible for Medicare Part A and Part B should enroll. In addition, MediGap insurance coverage is logical for a majority of people. Though a Medicare and MediGap combination has its limitations, it is still a great buy.

LONG-TERM CARE INSURANCE

Long-term care (LTC) insurance is probably the least enjoyable insurance to buy. Property and casualty insurance helps you restore the value of your property. Health insurance is used to restore your health. Even life insurance can later be cashed in or can serve as a "gift" to be passed on to your children. But LTC insurance is used to help you if you are unable to care for yourself because of prolonged illness or disability. And statistics show that there is a relatively high probability that you will spend time in a nursing home if you are sixty-five or older. Long-term care is a general term that includes everything from occasional help by non-medical personnel to around-the-clock medical assistance. Nursing home care can cost $36,000-$100,000 per year depending on the area of the United States and the quality of the facility. With life spans getting longer, the chances of spending time in a long-term care facility increases. Fifty percent of Americans who reach age eighty-five will need long-term care.

Long-term care is unique in that most retirement consultants believe it is not necessary for the poor or the rich. Those with less than $100,000 in net worth may find the premiums so costly that they cannot afford them. It would be disastrous to spend what little retirement savings you had on long-term care premiums and then not be able to pay the premiums (and therefore maintain the insurance) as you grow older. Not only would you have lost your long-term care coverage, but you would have wasted your retirement savings. People with a net worth of under $100,000 may also eventually qualify for Medicaid. On the other hand, people whose net worth is more than one million dollars should be able to self-finance their long-term care. If your net worth falls somewhere in between, you're probably a candidate for LTC insurance.

When To Buy

Late middle age — the late 50s or early 60s — is the best time to buy long-term care insurance. Purchasing LTC insurance prior to that will result in paying premiums for many years. On the other hand, at age sixty-five, premiums start to soar. Long-term care may cost as little as $400 per year in your 50s and as much as $4,000 per year in your 70s, depending on the type of coverage you choose.

What To Buy

First, you will want to buy a policy from a financially strong insurer that will be around if and when you need to collect the benefits. If you are under seventy, you should buy a policy that keeps pace with inflation even though it may cost you up to $1,000 per year more. If you feel you need long-term care insurance but must cut costs, the simplest way is to lengthen the elimination period, which can run from 0 to 180 days. The elimination period is the time it takes for your benefits to become effective. The longer you wait, the less expensive the policy. You may also want to limit the length of coverage to about five years in that 1) you may be able to pay some of your LTC expenses from savings and 2) the average nursing home stay is two and a half years. Ninety percent of all patients stay less than four years.

Long-term care policies vary from company to company. They are not regulated as MediGap insurance is. Be sure the LTC policy you choose provides adequate coverage for all levels of care from home care to skilled nursing care. Good policies also include guaranteed renewability, inflation-adjusted benefits, no prior hospitalization requirements, no exclusions for pre-existing conditions, and coverage in any health care setting.

Do I Need It At All?

Purchasing long-term care insurance is a good idea for those who have moderate retirement savings and can afford the premiums. There are, however, other factors to consider before purchasing long-term care insurance.

- Your family history. Everyone ages differently. If your family members tend to live longer and if they have used long-term care facilities, you may be more likely to want long-term care insurance.

- Your health condition. People with health problems that compromise their ability to care for themselves may consider getting long-term care insurance while they can still qualify.

- Help from family members. Some families stay in a close geographical location and others are far-flung. Some families maintain a tradition of caring for the senior members of their family. If you can estimate the amount of care you would receive from your family members, should you need it, it may help you decide on whether you need long-term care insurance, and if so, how much you need.

- Leaving assets to heirs. If you have a goal of leaving a significant estate to your heirs, you may want to purchase long-term care insurance to preserve your estate for the heirs.

PROPERTY AND LIABILITY INSURANCE

Because retirees have a fixed income, property and liability insurance is necessary to insure the ability to replace property and cover liabilities if disaster strikes. This type of insurance will cover the replacement of your home, cars, and other real estate. It will also protect you against loss from suits that may arise from accidents that have occurred on your property or as a result of your actions (or inactions). A few years ago, a major fire completely destroyed a beautiful home in a historic neighborhood. For many years, it had been the family home of a successful, now retired, dentist. In the course of interviewing the doctor about the tragic fire, the newspaper reporter learned that there was no insurance on the house. The doctor had discontinued the policy several years ago. When asked why he no longer carried insurance on the house, the doctor replied, "Because it was paid for, so I thought I didn't need to carry insurance any longer!" The doctor paid the tremendous cost of rebuilding the home.

Unlike the retired dentist, most senior citizens will not decide to drop coverage on a house or car. It's more likely that you will not have coverage because of a lapse in coverage, holes in your insurance coverage or an imbalance in your coverage. This is true both before and during retirement. As a result, you should meet with your insurance representative every few years and review your coverage.

Because we buy our insurance coverage at different times, we may tend to be over-insured in some areas and under-insured in others, making our coverage "out of balance." Consider the example of a couple who were married in their late 50s. Each owned an insured car, which they brought into the marriage. Since the policies were in place, they continued to pay the premiums as they came due. Each car was used equally by the couple. After five years of marriage, they reviewed their insurance coverage and found that one car had five times the liability coverage as the other. They also decided to drop the collision insurance on the older, second car because it was now becoming outdated.

UMBRELLA POLICY

Another inexpensive way to assure better coverage and avoid unpleasant surprises is to purchase an umbrella policy. An umbrella policy provides an extra $1-10 million of liability coverage on top of your house and car insurance and can be purchased for a few hundred dollars per year.

As we get older and our memory is not what it once was, some seniors put their insurance premiums on an automatic payment so valuable coverage does not lapse

While it's never much fun to pay for insurance, it does provide extra security for people who are past their major income earning years and need to protect their retirement savings and estate.

16
ASSET PROTECTION

When it comes to finances, no one has more interesting stories than attorneys who have seen millions of dollars of wealth disappear overnight because a person with wealth and without adequate asset protection became the target of a lawsuit. An asset protection attorney related this story to me only a few months ago:

He had recently counseled a chiropractor on several bankruptcy options — all of which could have been avoided if he had just planned ahead. A patient sued him for $3.5 million for a mistake he hadn't made. The patient had seen an orthopedic doctor immediately after a car accident and was released. After six weeks of treatment with the chiropractor she discharged herself, feeling healed. Nearly two and a half years later, she began litigation against the chiropractor because of a cancerous tumor on her spine — which the original physician had missed.

In their state, the statute of limitations for actions against medical doctors is two years, but for chiropractors, it's two and a half! Therefore, the chiropractor was the only one left to sue. Unfortunately, he had no asset protection in place, and to make matters worse, the court found that, for the purposes of this suit, he and his wife were still in partnership together, even though they had already separated their practices. That meant both his assets and those of his wife were subject to the judgment. Unfortunately, little can be done once a legal dispute begins.

HOW SAFE ARE YOU?

This scenario is becoming all too common and simple insurance policies are no longer enough. Liability may arise not only from professional malpractice, but also from personal injury, partnership liability, car accidents, accidents caused by your children or employees, equipment malfunctions, recreational accidents, divorce, discrimination, and sexual harassment claims. Recent evidence suggests that harassment and discrimination claims are becoming even more prevalent than malpractice claims. They are also much more difficult to defend. The good news is that, if you plan ahead, you can be protected.

Almost everyone protects their assets in one way or another. The amount of protection is usually relative to the size of the estate, the risk involved and the cost of protection.

• *Size of the estate.* One advantage of a small estate is that the cost of protection is usually simple and inexpensive. If your estate is comprised of a house, a car and a few thousand dollars of CDs in the bank, property and liability insurance on the house and the car may be all the asset protection you need. On the other hand, if you have a significant net worth — at least $250,000 — or plan to have a significant net worth in the future and are accumulating assets fairly rapidly, you may need significant asset protection.

• *Risk.* Some people, by virtue of their profession, their involvement in business or other factors, may be at exceptional risk for a lawsuit. People who serve on the board of directors with larger companies, doctors, dentists, small business owners and other high-risk endeavors, are prime candidates for a lawsuit. They are also prime candidates for increased asset protection.

• *Cost.* When we think of asset protection many think of insurance. But insurance alone is not enough if you have a significant estate. You will need other protection vehicles. And the cost of setting up and maintaining these protection vehicles can vary greatly depending on the type of protection you need and who you hire to create and maintain your protection entities.

Some people find adequate asset protection costs more than it's worth, but if you find the right asset protection plan and the right group of asset protection specialists, it can be relatively inexpensive and well worth the investment. Asset protection can no longer be viewed as a tool only for the ultra wealthy.

HIRING THE RIGHT TEAM

There are two key elements to hiring the right asset protection team (usually a law firm). First, hire a team that truly specializes in asset protection! Since it is such a narrow field of law, you will find that most good asset protection attorneys deal only in asset protection. Second, your asset protection team does not have to be a local group. My asset protection team, Lodmell & Lodmell, practices in Phoenix, Arizona. My wife and I live in the Midwest and Florida. Each year, we update our asset protection plan with one of the attorneys via a telephone conference. They also keep their clients up to date through their web site www.protectyourmoney.com.

Perhaps the most classic mistake made by people looking for advanced asset protection plans (beyond Wills, Trusts, etc.) is to use a local attorney who does not specialize in asset protection. Using a local attorney who specializes in divorce cases can be a major mistake. He may know very little about asset protection. And since people tend to be "down on" what they are not "up on," he may even discourage you from putting adequate asset protection in place.

Because protecting your assets and passing them on involves the input of your professional planners, you may find this chapter and the next (Chapter 17 — Passing Your Assets On) a little more difficult to understand. Don't worry about it — if you understand the basics, your professional planners will provide the details.

ASSET PROTECTION HELP

With good planning, you should be able to protect your entire estate. The proper structure does not need to be complicated or expensive, but it does need to be put in place before problems arise. A well-structured asset protection and estate plan can help you in several ways.

- It can avoid probate with its costly taxes and legal fees as well as frustrating delays in transferring your wealth to your heirs.
- It can preserve what is yours in the face of a court judgment after litigation.
- It will allow you to maintain control and privacy of your assets.
- You may pay reduced or no estate tax in some cases.
- You can pay for certain family expenses with dollars taxed at a lower rate.

What do you need for a secure estate plan? Several tools exist. Two of the most common, Wills and Trusts, will be discussed in the next chapter.

As your estate grows, you will want to have progressively more asset protection. Most people start out with the simplest/cheapest ideas. As their assets increase, they put more protection in place. Let's look at a common path.

JOINT TENANCY

Joint Tenancy is probably the simplest way of avoiding probate and protecting your assets. Joint Tenancy is a simple way you can share the ownership of a property equally with someone else (usually a husband and wife). If one owner dies, the surviving owner automatically becomes entitled to the property without probate. The property is also subject to probate when the last person dies.

Joint Tenancies are popular because they are simple and easy to understand. Joint Tenancies, however, can create problems. They are not a substitute for a Will. Because first, you may be giving up the opportunity to save taxes. Second, it's very difficult to own all your property in Joint Tenancy, and third, this form of ownership does not name a personal representative or guardian for your children.

LESS VISIBLE PARTY HOLDS TITLE

In the past — several decades ago — a common form of asset protection was simply to have the less visible party (the husband or the wife) hold assets in their name alone. If the husband owned a construction company and the wife worked only in the home, the couple would title their major assets in the wife's name only. The idea was that the husband, being the business owner, would be the most likely to be sued.

This form of asset protection may provide the smallest amount of protection, but it's easy to see that it is fraught with errors; it can create problems in the case of divorce and in passing the estate along to heirs, and can be penetrated very easily. It's probably more accurate to say that it provides a sense of asset protection, rather than actually providing much protection.

LIMITED LIABILITY COMPANIES

A Limited Liability Company (LLC) and other limited liability entities provide an excellent way to hold your risky investments, such as real estate, without jeopardizing your other investments. An LLC is a business entity that shields the members from liability much like a corporation but is taxed like a partnership. Today, real estate partnerships are much less common than they were in the past. LLCs have taken their place because of their simplicity and the asset protection that the LLC affords.

IRREVOCABLE LIFE INSURANCE TRUST

Most people think that life insurance proceeds are tax-free. This is true for income taxes, but not necessarily for estate taxes. The proceeds from a life insurance policy that you own when you die become part of your gross taxable estate — and subject to federal and state taxes. The taxes start at 37% and rise to 55% of a person's assets that are in excess of the unified credit exemption.

The solution is to create an Irrevocable Life Insurance Trust (ILIT). The Trust is the legal owner of the policy. The Trust also receives the proceeds as beneficiary under the policy. The use of Trusts today is very common and goes back for over a thousand years. In this case, the Trust's function is to hold the insurance policies. By using the Trust, both the surviving spouse and the children can be beneficiaries without worry of estate taxes. The Trust can support all the beneficiaries and ultimately distribute the death benefits to them tax-free. By using a Trust, you can create the maximum amount of flexibility and benefits, while insuring that you will not fall into the IRS trap and end up paying taxes on benefits that should be tax-free. But be careful — the insured must not have any "incidents of ownership" in the policy or it will go back into the estate.

REVOCABLE LIVING TRUST

The Revocable Living Trust (RLT) is probably the most common type of Trust today and should be one of the first steps taken in establishing any estate plan. The RLT will help you avoid probate and provide for two exemptions from federal estate taxes. Both functions are extremely important.

Avoiding probate can save thousands of dollars as costs may run as much as 3% of the estate's total assets. That means you could expect to pay $3,000 just to probate an estate of $100,000. Plus, during the probate process, your assets are frozen — usually for months, but possibly years — so that even your children or other beneficiaries cannot use them. The RLT avoids the entire probate process by placing all of the assets in a separate Trust unaffected by your death. You maintain complete control of all your assets until death and upon death, the person or persons you have identified as successor trustees will have immediate control of the Trust assets and can make distributions according to your instructions in the Trust.

The RLT also maintains significant federal estate tax exemption (increasing up to one million dollars by the year 2006). A Simple Will does not allow for that savings. This means you could save over $250,000 in estate taxes alone on a taxable estate of $1.25 million.

The good news is that you can achieve all this without ever giving up control of your assets. You can buy or sell as you see fit. You can even give your assets away. Best of all, your assets will be available immediately for your children or other heirs without the involvement of the courts.

IRREVOCABLE CHILDREN'S TRUST

The Irrevocable Children's Trust (ICT) is a unique planning device allowing you to reduce your overall taxes (by deducting expenses previously non-deductible) and pay for your children's "extraordinary" expenses with either tax-free dollars or dollars taxed at your children's lower rate.

These benefits are accomplished by setting up an Irrevocable Children's Trust with your children as the beneficiaries. Once the money is in the Trust, the Trust can begin paying your children's expenses, above and beyond basic support. That means the Trust can send your children to camp, purchase computers, or pay for private school or college. Depending on the age of your children, you can save thousands of dollars every year in taxes. It's an excellent way to protect your assets and pay less in taxes. It also removes those particular assets from your gross taxable estate and from the reach of any creditors.

FAMILY LIMITED PARTNERSHIP

The Family Limited Partnership (FLP) is a wonderful asset protection tool in use today. It should be used as part of a basic asset protection plan by anyone who is at high risk for lawsuits and who has a net worth of $300,000 or more. The FLP is a legal partnership established among family members for their — and your — benefit. When you're ready, you make a distribution of the cash or other assets in your FLP directly to yourself (as general partner) or to its "minority members."

Once your FLP is established, your "safe" assets are transferred into it. These include stocks, bonds, notes receivable, collectibles, cash and other safe assets. They are considered safe assets because they cannot injure anyone (and, as a result, subject the rest of your assets in the partnership to liability).

The advantages of an FLP are simple. First, any judgment against you personally will not attach to the FLP. The only remedy a creditor can obtain is a "charging order." This means only distributions made to you can be attached. The other members of the partnership are exempt! You maintain full control over the distributions, however, and no one can force you to make any distribution at all.

In considering a lawsuit, the best a creditor could hope for is to wait until the partnership is dissolved. In the meantime, the creditor would be liable for all the taxes due on your share of the undistributed income in the FLP. In other words, it would actually cost plaintiffs money just for a chance at your assets, even if they were to win in court. This roadblock alone — little prospect for a foreseeable payout — often deters would-be assailants and their lawyers.

The second significant benefit of the Family Limited Partnership is that it enables you to lower your estate taxes by using the "discount valuation" feature. This is possible because minority members own small percentages and because no real market for the shares exists. As a result, the IRS allows you to discount the value of your assets — often as much as 30% to 40%. Upon death, or if you give the shares of your FLP away, the assets are valued at this lower amount, therefore reducing your taxable estate. This could save you $200,000 or more in estate taxes alone! Remember, estate taxes start at 37% and sharply increase to 55%.

You can look at your Family Limited Partnership as a treasure chest, where all your assets will be locked up. It provides a formidable deterrent for anyone looking to force you into quick settlement or a drawn-out court proceeding. In addition, your FLP can serve as the cornerstone for your entire estate and asset protection plan by incorporating a real estate investment company and other investment vehicles.

INTERNATIONAL ASSET PROTECTION TRUST

If you have a large estate — a half million dollars or more — and/or are subject to significant risks for lawsuits, an International Asset Protection Trust (APT) may be the best way to protect your assets from unfounded lawsuits and illegitimate claims to your wealth. Used in conjunction with a Family Limited Partnership, an APT provides you the maximum barrier available to protect your assets. In case of real need, your assets will be physically removed to the jurisdiction of your choice, away from U.S. courts and judgments.

The APT should not be confused with an abusive offshore Trust that promises asset protection but is many times set up for the express purpose of avoiding taxes in the United States. They provide many legal concerns and targets for the IRS. The APT does not save or avoid taxes. Neither does it increase your tax potential. The APT is tax neutral.

The concept behind an Asset Protection Trust is simple. Instead of you or your Revocable Living Trust holding the majority interest in your Family Limited Partnership, your Asset Protection Trust (just as if it were a person) will hold it.

Should a situation occur where your assets are threatened, such as a lawsuit, the APT as an entity already "owns" most of the assets, which can be moved to another country, like Switzerland — outside the U.S. jurisdiction — and outside the reach of U.S. courts.

The offshore jurisdictions you use — perhaps Belize or the Cook Islands — will have enacted specific laws stating that they will recognize no court orders from any other country. As a result, regardless of the outcome in an U.S. court of law, your assets are safe.

In addition, since your APT owns the majority of your FLP, you can make distributions to the APT from your FLP assets. While the FLP alone provides mainly "deterrent" protection, the APT actually allows you to distribute your assets away from any claims to them.

An APT is recommended for those professional in a high risk occupation, such as doctors, dentists, chiropractors, lawyers, accountants, business owners, and anyone in partnership, whether it's business or personal (such as co-owning an airplane or boat). If you fit one of these categories and have a significant net worth, you are a prime candidate for a lawsuit and therefore, a prime candidate for an APT.

Another benefit of the APT is that it is considered a domestic "Grantor Trust" for U.S. tax purposes and is therefore tax neutral, which means there are no additional reporting requirements or tax returns to file, as long as assets remain in your U.S. Family Limited Partnership. And as a domestic Grantor Trust, it can hold title to your family residence and preserve the tax benefits, such as mortgage interest deductions and the $250,000 per person exemption from capital gains tax as well as your state's homestead exemption.

LIVING WILLS

Now that you have protected your assets against others, you may want to protect them against yourself! Unfortunately, many estates are devastated by the costs of providing life support and other around-the-clock care to someone who, if able to make a choice, would opt to be taken off life support. As a result, Living Wills have been created to address this issue.

Living Wills are documents that spell out exactly what methods should be taken and should not be taken to keep a person alive. According to the American Medical Association, 20% of all Americans now have a Living Will, and that number is rapidly growing. Your Living Will can probably be drawn up by your local attorney who handles your other basic estate planning. Having signed a Living Will, you should notify your spouse and children and keep it in a place that is immediately accessible. You may also want to give your primary physician a copy of your Living Will.

POWER OF ATTORNEY

Another way you can protect your assets in the event you become incapacitated is by giving someone else your "power of attorney." A power of attorney gives another person the legal right to act on your behalf. When you give them power of attorney, you are giving them the right to take care of your financial or legal matters, such as making investments, opening and closing accounts, and paying your bills. There are different types of attorney powers, such as general power of attorney, special power of attorney, standard power of attorney, durable power of attorney and springing durable power of attorney. Each provides a different level of "signing rights." Some allow your appointed person to act with power of attorney only in the case of your incompetence, others only for specific issues. You should discuss the powers of attorney with your personal attorney and choose the one that suits you best.

FRAUDS, SCAMS, AND MISUNDERSTANDINGS

There is more to true asset protection than Wills, Trusts, Family Limited Partnerships and Asset Protection Trusts. Many people, retirement age and beyond, fall prey to various frauds, scams, and misunderstandings.

• *Real Estate Deals.* If you live close to or visit a retirement community, you will certainly be fair game for con artists. They invite you to a dinner and show you beautiful slides of the future clubhouse, swimming pool, golfing greens and ready-to-build-on wooded lots. It's easy to catch the vision (that isn't there) and plunk down $35,000 on a lot that you've never seen — a lot with special assessments, unbuildable terrain, no water or sewer or even roads! Twelve years later, you'll be trying to sell the lot on your own for $3,000.

• *Abusive Trusts.* The IRS is going after both the promoters and the users of fraudulent Trust schemes. These schemes often promise to reduce or totally eliminate income tax, self-employment tax, deductions for personal expenses and the cost of your personal residence and furnishings. Further information can be found at www.irs.gov.

• *New Profession.* We've all heard stories about the retiree who found his "true profession" only after retirement. In most cases, you should be extremely careful about investing your retirement savings in the start up of a new business. This is especially important if you are being courted by a company that requires a large down payment for franchise rights or the purchase of large amounts of wholesale product to be resold in your new business. Once you find you have been misled, and that the $50,000 invested for "franchise rights" has little value, you may be faced with abandoning the idea and losing the $50,000 or seeking legal action for the return of the $50,000 — which may cost even more money!

• *Home Improvement Scams.* From time to time, every homeowner will need home improvements. But be careful of scam artists. Remember, home improvement contractors rarely go door to door looking for business! If home repair is needed, get at least three estimates from different contractors. If possible, work with someone you know and have used in the past with good results. Pay only after work has been completed. In the case of large projects, payments may need to be made on an installment basis. Be sure that the work is at the level of completion described in your agreement before dispersing funds.

• *Family Lending.* One of the easiest ways to erode your retirement assets is by providing financial help for family members. It is best to avoid loaning money to family members, but if you do make such loan, be sure to have the family member sign a note. If the loan goes unpaid, make that be a deterrent for future lending. A recent article in a sports magazine quoted one of basketball's highest paid athletes as saying he was virtually broke because he had lent money to various family members who were now unable to repay him. While it may be difficult to turn down repeated requests for financial assistance (even in the form of a loan) from close family members, it may be necessary to protect your retirement savings.

• *Banking Scams.* Never release your financial and credit card information to anyone who calls you by phone or contacts you in person no matter how urgent the request may appear! Financial scam artists use the forces of authority and urgency to dupe unsuspecting senior citizens. If you question the procedure at all, ask to have the opportunity to call them back at the bank or financial institution. Before you return the call, have your attorney or other advisors present on the call.

• *Discretionary Accounts.* Be careful of "slow motion" fraud. If you give your money managers the authority to invest your money as they see fit, you may fall victim to "the churning of accounts." This is a procedure where unethical investors buy and sell investments with your retirement savings — making money on every transaction. Each time, this churning eats up another portion of your retirement account. Giving an unscrupulous investor authority to buy and sell on your account is like hiring a fox to guard the hen house.

• *Misunderstanding Professional Advisors.* A common and innocent mistake made by many retirees is simply misunderstanding how your various financial advisors work for you. One older lady who had been recently widowed was disenchanted with her accountant because he had failed to provide her with good ideas for investing. She simply misunderstood the process. Investment advisors advise you on investments — accountants keep accounts. While your accountant may do a wonderful job of advising you on tax ideas based on the information you provide him, it is generally outside the accountant's role to search out good investment vehicles for his clients. Understanding your various advisors' roles will help you coordinate their activities and protect your investments.

As with insurance, proper asset protection planning can preserve your estate and give tremendous peace of mind. For asset protection to be valuable, it must be in place prior to the need. As you move toward retirement, you will want to assess the size of your estate and the risk of your assets and work with the appropriate asset protection specialists for maximum security in retirement.

PASSING YOUR ASSETS ON

T here are all kinds of unique stories about what happens to estates as they are passed from one generation to the next. In the past few years, I have witnessed three that have been quite unique.

Story 1: Lydia, a patient of mine, had reached the age where her own health should have been her main concern, but she was still busy caring for her 94-year-old uncle. He had lived on a farm as a widower for the past thirty years. His only living relative other than Lydia was his daughter, who lived eight hundred miles away and for all intents and purposes had disowned him because of a bitter argument decades before. Because his daughter refused to help in his care, the burden fell on Lydia.

Eventually, the farmer died without a Will, and his estate was passed on to his daughter. Whether it was because she had disowned her father, or felt guilty, or a combination of both, she refused to accept the inheritance. After a few years, the courts redirected the money, an estate worth nearly $400,000, to Lydia, the only other living relative. For years, Social Security had been her major source of income. Suddenly when she was in her early seventies, the value of her retirement account moved from zero to $400,000.

Story 2: Fred and May were married all of their adult life. She was ten years younger than Fred. Though they lived a fairly modest lifestyle, they had managed to put away a significant amount of money for retirement. Fred sold his business and placed the proceeds in his retirement account, and May had saved all the money she had made from thirty years of working outside the home and placed it in her retirement account. Soon after they retired, Fred's personality started to change. First, it was blamed on his unhappiness in retirement, then on a sleep disorder. But eventually he was diagnosed with Alzheimer's. May's life became consumed with caring for Fred — never once thinking about asset protection. Now, Fred has been in a nursing home for years, and although Fred and May always kept their retirement accounts separate, the state looks at them as one. May now faces the fact that the cost of Fred's long-term care may consume both of their retirement savings accounts while she is still in early retirement.

Story 3: Follow this story carefully as it's confusing! Edward and Evelyn were married at a young age. They had two boys who helped in the family business while they were young and then moved on to start their own businesses. Even before retirement, Evelyn died of an aneurysm. After a few years, Edward remarried. As a couple, they had a Simple Will drawn up by a local attorney. The estate would be left in its entirety to the surviving spouse. Within a matter of months, Edward developed a brain tumor and died. His estate went to Gertrude, his new wife. After a few more years, Gertrude remarried Edward's brother, Henry, who had virtually no assets. They, too, had a Simple Will drawn up. After a few years, Gertrude died leaving the estate to Henry. Henry then died, leaving the estate — most of which had been amassed by Edward — to his own children, which meant that the inheritance that would have normally passed from Edward to his children was instead passed to Henry's children — Edward's cousins!

PLEASE PASS THE ASSETS

The first step in passing your assets on is simply providing an organized account of all your assets, liabilities and business documents. Imagine your family's situation at your death. Surviving family members have to take over your complex financial activities, locate all your assets, locate Wills and other documents, pay debts, value estate assets, make death claims — the list goes on and on. It's not surprising that bank accounts often go unclaimed, insurance death claims aren't filed and probate is slow and costly! These problems can be reduced or eliminated simply by taking time to list your assets and their locations. To do this, you will need a written record of your personal and financial information and information on where to locate your important documents. The Written Records Document found in Appendix A was provided by my personal attorney to assist in recording the information that may be needed by heirs and executors. Each year, during the last week of the year, my wife and I update our written records. Completing the enclosed Written Records Document and informing your heirs of its location may be the single most important action you can take to facilitate the passing of your assets.

In addition to these Written Records Document, you need a Document Locator, which is, as it sounds, simply a place where you keep all important documents. This Document Locator may be as simple as an accordion file with the following divisions:

ESTATE PLANNING GUIDE

1. PERSONAL DATA
Birth certificates, passports, death certificates, voter registration, Social Security Cards

2. PERSONAL PROPERTY
Car titles, household inventory/receipts, lifestyle/luxury item receipts

3. INVESTMENTS
Checking/savings accounts, money market funds, CDs, bonds, stocks, mutual funds, etc.; notes receivable from others, land contracts

4. RETIREMENT
IRAs, pension/profit sharing/SEP, tax shelters, annuities

5. INSURANCE
Liability/malpractice/health/auto/disability/life/homeowners/long-term care

---

6. REAL ESTATE

Deeds & improvement receipts, land contracts, title insurance/abstracts, commercial property & improvement receipts, vacation/second home & improvement receipts

7. INDEBTEDNESS

Mortgages, Deeds of Trust, bank loans/notes, personal/family loans, car loans, installment loans

8. ESTATE PLANNING

Wills, Trust Instruments

9. MISCELLANEOUS

Your Document Locator should be placed in a fireproof safe or other secure location.

HIRING A PROFESSIONAL

Some retirement "experts" suggest that you can save money by writing your own Will. I hope you're not foolish enough to take them seriously! This is not a do-it-yourself project. Writing a Will (or other retirement documents) is not work for the amateur. In fact, you will want to use attorneys who specialize in estate planning! Don Bowman, of Bowman and Krieger in Lincoln, Nebraska, is the author of the Written Records Document on the previous pages and an expert in estate planning. According to Mr. Bowman, less than 50% of adults over 30 years old have Wills.

Before choosing an estate lawyer, speak with at least three. Find someone who is knowledgeable and can explain estate planning in simple terms. You may also want to get references from others who have worked with them.

YOUR WILL

Some of the documents you use to *protect* your assets (found in the previous chapter) are also used to *pass* on your assets to your heirs. As a result, we talked about them in detail in Chapter 16 and will discuss them here only briefly. On the other hand, a Will is used to determine what will be done with your assets upon death and is the core of many estate distribution plans.

A Will is your opportunity to do what *you* want with *your* estate. Don't let outside sources tell you what you want. If you do not execute a Will, your state law will determine who gets your property and when they will receive it. The major drawback to the state's distribution plan is that your property probably won't go to those you want to receive it. The state's "one size fits all" distribution plan has some clear disadvantages:

- Your property may be divided between your spouse and your children; your spouse may not receive all your assets.

- Your children will be entitled to their share of your estate when they reach the age of majority, even though they may not have the ability to handle it properly.

- You will lose the opportunity to choose your own executor and your children's guardian.

- You will lose many opportunities to save taxes and minimize costs.

By executing a Will, you avoid all these problems. It lets you design a distribution plan tailor-made to your needs.

Simple Will

With a Simple Will, the entire estate passes outright to the surviving spouse. If there is no surviving spouse, the entire estate will go to the children. Such a Will is probably best if your estate is not large and you do not feel that either your spouse or children need financial supervision.

A Simple Will with a Trust for the children are also commonly used for relatively modest estates. With this type of Will, you leave everything to your spouse if living at your death. If your spouse is not living at your death, your Will creates a Trust for the benefit of your children. The trustee will manage the property, as you direct in your Will, for the benefit of the children. The trustee can be either a Trust department in a bank or an individual.

Tax Saving Will

If your estate is large enough that federal estate taxes may be due, you should consider a Tax Saving Will. Changes in the federal estate tax law allow many Americans to avoid paying this tax altogether if they plan properly. There are two tax breaks available to you. First, there is no federal estate tax due on property you leave to your spouse. This so-called "marital deduction" will allow postponement of the federal estate tax until your spouse's death. Second, you will be allowed to leave up to $1,000,000 to anyone without paying federal estate tax when these new provisions became totally effective. In 2006, with proper planning, a husband and wife will be able to leave up to $2,000,000 tax-free.

Proper use of these two tax breaks can save a tremendous amount of money. For example, if you have a $1.35 million estate and leave everything to your spouse, there will be no taxes due upon your death. But when your spouse dies, $235,000 in taxes will have to be paid on the $1.35 million estate. If, however, you leave $675,000 to a "Bypass Trust" for your family and $675,000 to your spouse, there would be no taxes due at either death. Obviously, the right kind of Will can save a lot in taxes.

Under the most popular Tax Saving Will, you make the maximum possible tax-free bequest to your children, or to a Trust for the benefit of your children. (Remember, the law allows you to give $675,000 to your children without federal estate taxes.) The balance of your estate goes to your spouse or to a Trust for your spouse. (Remember, no federal estate tax is paid on property left to your spouse.) Such a Will is designed to transfer as much property as possible to the children at the first death without the payment of any federal estate taxes.

Another popular Tax Saving Will leaves half your estate to your children (or to a Trust for your children) and half your estate to your spouse (or a Trust for your spouse). Depending on the size of your estate, this Will arrangement may produce estate tax at your death. However, the taxes due at your spouse's eventual death will generally be less than under the first form of Tax Saving Will. You should consult with your attorney and other tax advisors to determine which form of Tax Saving Will is best for you.

Regardless of which form of Tax Saving Will is used, the property that goes to the children is generally put in Trust. The Trust can be written to give your spouse substantial rights in the property but still avoid taxation in his or her estate.

The property going to the surviving spouse is also often placed in Trust for two reasons. First, the Trust will save probate expenses at the death of the surviving spouse, and second, the Trust can provide professional investment management.

JOINT TENANCY

In the last chapter we discussed Joint Tenancy and Trusts. Joint Tenancy is probably the simplest way of avoiding probate. Joint Tenancy is simply a way you can share the ownership of property equally with someone else. If one owner dies, the surviving owner automatically becomes entitled to the property without probate.

Probate is the court-supervised process under which a deceased person's assets are gathered and disbursed. In many circumstances, avoiding probate is to your advantage. You can avoid probate in three ways: through jointly owned property; through life insurance and other property that is paid to a named beneficiary; and through a Revocable Trust.

TRUSTS

Again, you can control the distribution of your property outside of the probate process by creating a Trust. In fact, a special kind of Trust — called a Revocable Trust — is sometimes used as a substitute for a Will. Unlike a Will, a Revocable Trust acts on your property without probate.

A Trust is simply a separation of legal and beneficial ownership. That is, the trustee is the legal owner of the Trust property but does not own it for his or her own benefit. Instead, the trustee must use the property exclusively for the benefit of the Trust beneficiaries — usually your family. What the trustee can do with the property depends on the terms of the "Trust document" which you, with the help of your attorney, write. For example, the Trust document might say that the trustee will use the Trust property to pay for your children's health care and education.

Revocable Trusts, however, are not for everyone.

• It's easy to overestimate the savings from a Revocable Trust. Remember that you will have to pay someone to draft the Trust. Furthermore, there will be some expenses at death despite the Trust. For example, tax returns will still need to be prepared and filed, and a Revocable Trust does not avoid estate or inheritance taxes.

• The Revocable Trust is one more financial item to worry about while you're living.

• Sometimes, probate can offer income tax advantages not available with a Revocable Trust.

Trusts for Minor Children

A Trust can contain provisions for the care of your children before they become of age (and thereafter if you choose), avoiding the expense and inconvenience of guardianship and conservatorship. A Pour-Over Will to a Trust is an excellent arrangement for minor children where no parent is surviving.

Be careful in setting up your Trusts and Will. Your property owner-ship and insurance designations should be properly coordinated with your Will. As we've discussed, jointly held property and life insurance generally pass outside your Will. Occasionally, people execute sophisti-cated Tax Savings Wills but own almost all their property in Joint Tenancy. In such cases, their property ownership defeats the purpose of their Will.

Irrevocable Life Insurance Trust

An Irrevocable Life Insurance Trust is designed to save your family federal estate taxes. The best way to understand how it works is to con-sider an example. Suppose you own insurance on your life, payable to your spouse. On your death, there will be no federal estate tax on the insurance. (Remember, you're allowed to transfer an unlimited amount of property to your spouse without federal estate tax.) However, when your spouse dies, any of the insurance proceeds he or she has not spent will be in his or her estate where they will be exposed to the federal estate tax.

Suppose, instead, that you transfer ownership of your insurance to an Irrevocable Life Insurance Trust. Since you don't own the insurance, the insurance won't be in your estate (assuming it was in your Trust for three years before your death). Furthermore, the attorney can draft the Trust so it won't be included in your spouse's estate, even though the spouse is given substantial rights to the Trust.

How much money an Irrevocable Trust can save your family depends on the size of your estate. However, the minimum federal estate tax bracket is 37% on every insurance dollar or $37,000 on a $100,000 insurance policy. This makes the cost to set up the Trust seem very rea-sonable.

When should you consider an Irrevocable Trust? In general, you should consider an Irrevocable Trust if your estate, including the face amount of your insurance, is more than:

- $1,350,000 if married (eventually escalates to $2,000,000 by 2006)
- $675,000 if single (eventually escalates to $1,000,000 by 2006)

Remember that the Irrevocable Trust is needed only for larger estates. Smaller estates can avoid all federal estate taxes even without an Irrevocable Trust.

BUY/SELL AGREEMENTS

If you own a business, it may be the biggest single asset in your estate. You and your family probably depend on it for income. If you die, unless some family member is capable of taking over the business, the business income will stop. Your family will, therefore, probably try to sell the business. But your family may not be in a position to negotiate a good price because potential purchasers know that your family has to sell. Therefore, most of the value you've built up over the years will simply vanish.

The solution is to negotiate a good price for your business now, while you're in a strong bargaining position. This can be done through a buy/sell agreement. Most commonly, buy/sell agreements are entered into between business partners. For example, suppose you own a business with a partner. You and your partner agree that if you die, he will buy your family out (buy the business) at a pre-determined price. You also agree to buy his family out if he dies before you do. If you have no business partner, consider entering into a buy/sell agreement with a key employee, or perhaps even a competitor.

Be sure the buy/sell agreement is kept with your other legal documents (in your Document Locator) so it is not overlooked by your executor.

A PERSONAL REPRESENTATIVE

Your Personal Representative (also known as an "Executor") will collect and protect your assets, pay the debts of your estate and distribute what's left over to your heirs. This sounds simple, but the entire process can entail as many as 60 to 70 separate steps. The first thing your executor must do is to locate and read your Will. This should be easy if you have a Document Locator. Next, your Personal Representative will take your Will to the Probate Court and attempt to prove the Will valid.

Your Personal Representative's most challenging duties will involve collecting and preserving your assets. Your Personal Representative will locate and inventory all your assets. His or her job will be easier if you've filled out the Written Records Document found earlier in this chapter. Your Personal Representative will take title of all bank accounts and securities in the name of your estate. Your Personal Representative will also have to set up a checking account and record system. All money due your estate must be collected. This will include making insurance claims, filing claims for veteran benefits and Social Security benefits, and similar items. He must also obtain adequate insurance coverage and maintain your property since he is responsible for protecting your assets.

Your Personal Representative must also pay off all estate debts. Your creditors will have approximately three months to make their claims. If your estate is large enough, a federal estate tax will be payable. Some states also have an inheritance and/or estate tax. The expenses of pro-bating and administering your estate must also be paid. Your Personal Representative will also have to file income tax returns for both you and your estate. All this will cost money. It may be necessary to liquidate estate assets to pay for all these items.

After all the debts have been paid, your Personal Representative will distribute whatever remains and make a final accounting to the court. At this point, if everything is in order, your Personal Representative will be discharged. This will take months and perhaps even more than a year.

Choosing A Personal Representative

First, decide whether to use a corporate Personal Representative, such as a bank's Trust department, or an individual. A corporate Personal Representative is familiar with the probate process, can handle

the many complexities of the probate process properly, and has perpetu-
al existence. That is, unlike an individual, it won't get sick, it won't die,
and it won't be on vacation when a death occurs. If an individual
Personal Representative dies or becomes seriously ill during probate, the
process can be seriously disrupted. Finally, don't forget that a Personal
Representative can be held liable to the heirs for mistakes. It may be
inadvisable to subject your family members to this liability.

Before naming a corporate Personal Representative, make sure the
particular bank or Trust department is willing to administer your estate.
Some banks or Trust departments will not administer an estate unless it
exceeds a certain size. In addition, your Will might contain a provision,
such as retaining a family business during the probate process, that a corporate trustee would not be willing to administer. Also check out the
corporate Personal Representative's fee structure and investment track
record. Finally, try to determine how sensitive the bank will be to your
family's needs.

Despite the many advantages of choosing a corporate Personal
Representative, many people name family members as Personal
Representatives. Some people feel that a family member may be more
sensitive to the needs of the family than a corporate trustee and family
members often serve without compensation. A family member, though,
will almost certainly have to hire an attorney to handle the probate
process, so the actual savings may be less than expected. Before naming
a family member as your Personal Representative, ask yourself the following questions: Is the family member in good health? Is the family
member responsible? Is this family member capable of administering the
estate? Does the family member have sufficient time to handle estate
affairs? Will other family members be offended that they were not
named?

Attorneys and accountants are sometimes named as Personal
Representatives. To avoid misunderstanding, you should decide
whether the attorney or accountant will receive compensation both as
the Personal Representative and as the attorney or accountant for the

estate.

SPECIFIC INSTRUCTIONS

According to some tax attorneys, the biggest problem in settling estates is often the children fighting over "stuff." A good Will addresses this problem.

INSTRUCTIONS OUTSIDE YOUR WILL

There are some things that you should not put in your Will. For example, your Will generally should not give guidance or state wishes. Such languages could be confused with bequests. Also, your Will is generally a public document and there may be some information you wish to convey privately to your family. For these reasons, an informal letter to your family can be an extremely helpful and appropriate supplement to your Will.

The letter to your family can include:

• Steps to be followed immediately after your death
• Your motives for certain Will provisions
• Suggestions for handling special estate assets such as stamp or coin collections
• Recommendations on financial advisors
• Funeral and burial instructions

REVIEW YOUR WILL

Some people write a Will and never review it. Their family has changed, their estate has grown, and their wishes have changed, but the outdated Will stays intact. Your Will should be reviewed if:

• There has been a substantial change in the value of your estate
• You have inherited property
• There have been births, deaths, divorces, or marriages that affect the

Will disposition
- You have moved to another state
- The executor can no longer serve
- A new guardian of minors must be selected
- More than three years has passed since the last review

NON-FINANCIAL ASSETS

We've all heard the saying, "Give a man a fish; he'll eat for a day. Teach him to fish, and he will eat forever." We should remember that properly passing our financial assets to the next generation (or whomever you determine) is only a small portion of what we actually pass on. Our customs, traditions, spiritual beliefs, work ethic, and savings habits may also be passed on. You may want to hold an annual family conference to discuss these items and pass the responsibility for maintaining traditions to younger family members as you move into retirement. Finally, much of the ability to pass on family values will be contained in our actions. Stewardship, discipline, goal setting, and advanced planning are characteristics that are passed on best when accompanied by example. You may want to involve the next generation in your retirement planning; at least to the extent that they understand why you have made your decisions and what you hope to accomplish throughout your retirement.

18

STAYING HAPPY
THROUGHOUT RETIREMENT

Michael Jordan isn't the only basketball player on the planet — Jimmy Reeder plays, too!

It's the Olympic Games. Jimmy and the team make another run for the Gold. However, unlike Michael Jordan, Jimmy's name is not a household word. Perhaps that is because it's the Senior Olympics — Jimmy Reeder is 70 years old.

His team is defeated again, but he just smiles. He'll try again during the next Olympics!

Jimmy and his wife, Billie, are the embodiment of perfect retirement. As an elementary school principal, and later as an elected member of the Tulsa Public School Board, Jimmy threw his heart into teaching — through profession and by example. Billie used her graduate degree as a teacher, too.

At ages 57 and 55, they retired, Jimmy to a second career selling pre-paid legal services and Billie as a volunteer at least one day a week at a museum and two days a week working for the Tulsa Assistance League — an organization that provides new clothing for needy children. They continue to have fun together — it's hard to catch them without a smile. Time is divided appropriately between family, grandchildren, church, work, and fun. Two nights ago they showed us pictures of their recent trip to Europe — nearly a month long — planned in advanced and executed almost flawlessly. As I listened to them recap the adventure, I realized that the true test of successful retirement is not the amount of money saved but the amount of happiness produced.

SEEING INTO THE FUTURE

Retirement, like life, ends up best if we know what we want in advance. If we can see into the future, we can begin with the end in mind. Unfortunately, it's not always easy to look ahead and predict what will bring happiness in our retirement years. As a result, we may get sidetracked, possibly for years, with roadblocks, obstacles, and detours that pull us off course. The dream of foreign travel can be usurped by paying for a degenerative hip surgery! The idea of having a second home on the lake doesn't materialize because our stock portfolio has performed so poorly. And the happiness we anticipated in watching our grandchildren grow seems almost out of reach now that their parents have divorced and the kids are living a thousand miles away.

HANDLING OBSTACLES AND ROAD BLOCKS

Without being pessimistic we can reasonably expect some problems throughout retirement. In fact, they may come with more frequency than during pre-retirement. And while we can't stop the problems from coming, we can minimize their effects by dealing with them efficiently.

First, don't adopt the attitude that "I'll just have to live with it" — at least not yet! One of the disadvantages of learning from history is that as our paradigm changes, we still use our old solutions to solve today's new problems. Compare your generation to those people who retired just 40 years ago. They could expect to spend only one-fifth as much time in retirement as you! Many had jobs that simply wore out their bodies, and they expected to be old and decrepit at retirement! We should also remember that the health care of 40 years ago cannot compare to the advanced health care available today. As a result, we can't afford to think like the retirees of 40 years ago, and we can't adopt their "I'll just have to live with it" mentality. We cannot consign ourselves to the idea that as we get older, these lifestyle limiting changes are inevitable — at least not to the extent that some of us are willing to accept.

So how do we combat the mentality of the past generation? Here are some ideas:

• **Demand attention.** Unfortunately, a large segment of our population — health care providers included — are perfectly willing to accept the fact that older people "just have to live with it." But that's not true. We will not be relegated to the back of the line. As an ever-growing group of consumers, we need to bring attention to any area of the market where we are treated differently than other consumers. When your doctor blames health care conditions on your age, suggests that they are "normal" for older people, and that you may have to "expect" these types of things in the future…instead of it signaling that you may have to change your lifestyle, it should signal that you may want to change doctors!

• **Take the corrective action.** Not all the problems we decide to live with are the result of other people's thoughts and actions. Many times we know what corrective action is needed, but are hesitant to take it. Why blame your broker for a continued bad ROI on your mutual funds? You can change mutual funds — or even stockbrokers — as easy as the 35-year-old investor. You must simply take the action. Why wait until all the color and life have gone out of your vision before cataract surgery? Why put up with things that can be corrected? We can't blame others for our inactions.

• **Do your part.** Perhaps the biggest deterrent to living a full life in retirement is inaction *on our part.* As with everything in nature, when we take the path of least resistance, we tend to run downhill. How can a 60-year-old retiree complain of body stiffness and limited ranges of motion when he doesn't even exercise? How can we complain about being left behind by society when we haven't been on the Internet or read a book since the day we retired? How can we complain about "not getting out much anymore" when we've never planned a trip? In other words, we are ultimately responsible for overcoming our obstacles and pushing through the roadblocks.

CONSIGNED TO MEDIOCRITY

Another common challenge for retirees is maintaining an active enough lifestyle for their place in retirement. I can understand why an 82-year-old's exercise routine would be a casual walk in the evening. But, what about the 55-year-old retiree? A casual walk three times a week? I don't think so! Even a brisk walk should be reserved for after 55. Before 55, you should still be competing in road races or at least doing fun runs!

Your mind also needs appropriate exercise. Surfing the Net, reading books, public speaking, writing, and even part-time jobs keep us sharp. Before we complain about others consigning us to "old-age retirement," let's make sure we haven't done it to ourselves. If we demand more from our minds and our bodies, we will probably comply.

IF YOU DO HAVE TO LIVE WITH IT

We're not living in a vacuum. We all realize that eventually there may be constraints that may indeed limit our retirement lifestyle. We've all heard of the concept of growing old gracefully. Unfortunately, some older people confuse that with the command, "Roll over and play dead." Growing old gracefully does not mean laying back and letting time take its course. Perhaps the best way to grow old gracefully is to fight it every step of the way, and then (and only then) gracefully accept the changes that occur. There's no reason to move — gracefully or ungracefully — into a sedentary life because of a degenerative hip, when a simple hip replacement surgery could put you back in circulation again.

Once we are truly confronted with physical or other limitations, we still have the opportunity to live our life to the fullest within those given limitations. The last freedom we lose is the freedom to dream within given parameters. Regardless of our future limitations, we still have a choice to be our best within those limitations.

GOALS THAT CREATE HAPPINESS

Everyone has goals, and it's a generally accepted thought that when we reach our goals, we will be happy. That's not always true. Sometimes we work for goals that, when reached, are not fulfilling. As a result, we're successful in reaching goals, but not happy. In retirement, as throughout life, long-term happiness occurs not when we reach goals but when we stay true to our values. If one of your major values in life is nurturing the family, then goals such as family vacations, successful parenting activities, becoming involved in your children's athletic events, and helping them establish good study habits are goals that support one of your major values. These goals will provide long-term satisfaction and happiness. On the other hand, let's assume you had those same family values and did not have strong business values, but because of the hectic work pace, you set goals for working longer hours, completing business projects, earning more pay, and receiving a promotion. The accomplishment of these goals would provide temporary pleasure but not long-term satisfaction. Why? Because these goals did not support your values. Happiness occurs when we are taking actions to reach our goals that support our values.

"Reaching goals" in and of itself does not necessarily bring happiness. Only when your goals support your values does your life become fulfilled — happy. Reaching goals that do not support your core values may give transient pleasure — but there's a big difference between pleasure and happiness. In fact, sometimes we must say "no" to the pleasures of the day so we can say "yes" to the happiness of a lifetime. It would be nice to stay late at work and finish a project early, but it does not support your core value (family). That good feeling of getting the project done on time will soon evaporate. Reaching goals that do not support your values is like climbing the steps of a ladder only to find that it's leaning against the wrong building. On the other hand, taking actions that lead to the accomplishment of goals, that support your values, provides happiness. You must first review your values, then set your goals accordingly, and take action.

If one of your core values involves a good spiritual life, it may follow that some of your goals may include volunteering at your church, singing in the choir, or leading a fellowship group. If during the day you take actions accordingly, such as going to choir practice or manning a telephone prayer line, you will feel fulfilled and happy.

Perhaps the best way to find happiness in retirement is to take action each day on goals that support your values.

A TIME FOR CHANGE

Retirement provides so many wonderful opportunities! Now *you* can concentrate on what *you* want to do. Before retirement, the pressures of creating an adequate income, supporting the work of your company, and struggling to accumulate a retirement savings may have caused you to put some of your interests — even your most important interests — on hold.

A decade ago, I was vacationing on the coast. It was mid-morning and I had left the condo for a run on the beach. I love setting and reaching goals — so much so that I had written my goals in the order of their importance (perhaps urgency) on the back of a business card, to carry with me. As I ran down the beach, I would simply glance down at each goal and then formulate a plan of action for reaching that goal. Over a two-mile stretch, I had pretty much reviewed the entire list, from most to least important.

As I approached the turn-around point, I noticed two surfers sitting on their boards out in the ocean and motioning for a lifeguard while pointing to something floating in the water. It didn't seem to be a person in distress in that the surfers were in no hurry to help, and when the lifeguard reached them in the water, he simply turned to the shore and motioned for another lifeguard for assistance. Perhaps it was just a significant piece of debris. As the lifeguards made their way back to shore, what they were dragging through the water became identifiable. It was indeed a human body. It had apparently been dead so long that there was no need to attempt resuscitation.

As I started my run back, with my goals still in hand — realizing the fragility of life — the importance of my goals seemed to change. In fact, in lieu of what I had just witnessed, it seemed that the list was almost upside down! Things on the top of the list, like "purchasing a new building," now seemed far less important than those on the bottom — "spend some quality time with my son before he graduates and leaves home."

If there's ever a time to put things in perspective, it's as you enter your retirement years. You are now out of the business rat race. You no longer have to earn more money. Many of the "urgencies" are gone. Now it's time to concentrate on the "important" things in life. While your business and financial matters may have been very time- and energy-consuming during your work years, they will now naturally segue to the importance of your family life, spiritual life, and other important matters. I doubt that there are many people who on their deathbed say, "I wish I would have spent more time at the office!"

We are indeed a blessed group. No generation in history has been able to retire in comfort and happiness like we are. No generation has had a longer expected retirement. No country has provided more opportunity and support for the retired. And because of the baby boomer generation, we are hitting retirement with enough critical mass to impact society's response to our needs. We are, perhaps the first generation who can truly have it all.

APPENDIX A

WRITTEN RECORDS DOCUMENT

HUSBAND

Full Name: _____

Telephone Number : _____

Known by Any Other Name: _____

Address:_____

E-mail Address: _____ Password: _____

Domicile: _____ Vote Where: _____

Auto Tags Where: _____ State Income Tax Paid Where: _____

Date of Birth: _____ Place of Birth: _____

Location of Birth Certificate: _____

Occupation: _____ Annual Income: _____

Previous Marriages: _____

State of Health: _____ Insurable: _____

WIFE

Full Name: _____

Telephone Number : _____

Known by Any Other Name: _____

Address:_____

E-mail Address: _____ Password: _____

Domicile: _____ Vote Where: _____

Auto Tags Where: _____ State Income Tax Paid Where: _____

Date of Birth: _____ Place of Birth: _____

Location of Birth Certificate: _____

Occupation: _____ Annual Income: _____

Previous Marriages: _____

State of Health: _____ Insurable: _____

CHILDREN

Is there a possibility of more children? _____

Are any children adopted? _____

Have any children been placed for adoption? _____

Are any children handicapped or in poor health? _____

1. Child's Name: _____ Date of Birth: _____

Child's Parent(s)_____

Address: _____

Education: _____

Business Ability: _____

Occupation:_____ Net Worth:_____ Annual Income: _____

Child's Spouse's Name:_____

Occupation: _____ Annual Income:_____

Child's Children:_____ Age: _____

_____ Age: _____

_____ Age: _____

Comments:_____

2. Child's Name: _____ Date of Birth: _____

Child's Parent(s)_____

Address: _____

Education: _____

Business Ability: _____

Occupation:_____ Net Worth:_____ Annual Income: _____

Child's Spouse's Name: _____

Occupation: _____ Annual Income:_____

Child's Children:_____ Age: _____

_____ Age: _____

_____ Age: _____

Comments:_____

3. Child's Name: _____ Date of Birth: _____

Child's Parent(s)_____

Address: _____

Education: _____

Business Ability: _____

Occupation:_____ Net Worth:_____ Annual Income: _____

Child's Spouse's Name: _____

Occupation: _____ Annual Income:_____

Child's Children:_____ Age: _____

_____ Age: _____

_____ Age: _____

Comments: _____

4. Child's Name: _____ Date of Birth: _____

Child's Parent(s)_____

Address: _____

Education: _____

Business Ability: _____

Occupation:_____ Net Worth:_____ Annual Income: _____

Child's Spouse's Name: _____

Occupation: _____ Annual Income:_____

Child's Children:_____ Age: _____

_____ Age: _____

_____ Age: _____

Comments: _____

HUSBAND'S PARENTS

	FATHER	MOTHER
Name:	_____	_____
Address:	_____	_____
Age:	_____	_____
State of Health:	_____	_____
Financially Dependent?	_____	_____

WIFE'S PARENTS

Name:	_____	_____
Address:	_____	_____
Age:	_____	_____
State of Health:	_____	_____
Financially Dependent?	_____	_____

ANY EXPECTED INHERITANCES?

	HUSBAND	WIFE
From Whom:	_____	_____
Approximate Value:	_____	_____
From Whom:	_____	_____
Approximate Value:	_____	_____

BROTHERS AND SISTERS

Name: _____ Living: _____

Age: _____ Married: _____ Children: _____

Comments: _____

Name: _____ Living: _____

Age: _____ Married: _____ Children: _____

Comments: _____

Name: _____ Living: _____

Age: _____ Married: _____ Children: _____

Comments: _____

Name: _____ Living: _____

Age: _____ Married: _____ Children: _____

Comments: _____

SPOUSE'S BROTHERS AND SISTERS

Name: _____ Living: _____

Age: _____ Married: _____ Children: _____

Comments: _____

Name: _____ Living: _____

Age: _____ Married: _____ Children: _____

Comments: _____

Name: _____ Living: _____

Age: _____ Married: _____ Children: _____

Comments: _____

Name: _____ Living: _____

Age: _____ Married: _____ Children: _____

Comments: _____

OTHER FAMILY INFORMATION

_____

_____

_____

_____

_____

FINANCIAL ADVISORS

ATTORNEY

Name: _____ Address:_____

_____ Phone:_____

ACCOUNTANT

Name: _____ Address:_____

_____ Phone:_____

ASSET PROTECTION SPECIALIST

Name: _____ Address:_____

_____ Phone:_____

INSURANCE

Property & Casualty

Name: _____ Address:_____

_____ Phone:_____

Life Insurance

Name: _____ Address:_____

_____ Phone:_____

Auto Insurance

Name: _____ Address:_____

_____ Phone:_____

Other

Name: _____ Address:_____

_____ Phone:_____

TRUST OFFICER

Name: _____ Address: _____

_____ Phone: _____

INVESTMENTS

Name: _____ Address: _____

_____ Phone: _____

BANKER

Name: _____ Address: _____

_____ Phone: _____

PERSONAL REPRESENTATIVE

Name: _____ Address: _____

_____ Phone: _____

TRUSTEE

Name: _____ Address: _____

_____ Phone: _____

GUARDIAN

Name: _____ Address: _____

_____ Phone: _____

SPECIAL RELATIVES OR FRIENDS

Name: _____ Address: _____

_____ Phone: _____

OTHER ADVISORS

Name: _____ Address: _____

_____ Phone: _____

Name: _____ Address: _____

_____ Phone: _____

Name: _____ Address: _____

_____ Phone: _____

Name: _____ Address: _____

_____ Phone: _____

Name: _____ Address: _____

_____ Phone: _____

Name: _____ Address: _____

_____ Phone: _____

CREDIT CARD INVENTORY

CARD & CARD NUMBER	CARD ISSUER	PHONE

HOUSEHOLD INVENTORY

Videotape of house contents is located: _____

KITCHEN

ITEM	PURCHASE DATE	PURCHASE PRICE
_____	_____	$ _____
_____	_____	$ _____
_____	_____	$ _____
_____	_____	$ _____
_____	_____	$ _____
_____	_____	$ _____
_____	_____	$ _____

DINING ROOM

_____	_____	$ _____
_____	_____	$ _____
_____	_____	$ _____
_____	_____	$ _____
_____	_____	$ _____
_____	_____	$ _____
_____	_____	$ _____

LIVING ROOM

_____	_____	$ _____
_____	_____	$ _____
_____	_____	$ _____
_____	_____	$ _____
_____	_____	$ _____
_____	_____	$ _____
_____	_____	$ _____

BEDROOM #1

ITEM	PURCHASE DATE	PURCHASE PRICE
		$
		$
		$
		$
		$
		$
		$

BEDROOM #2

		$
		$
		$
		$
		$
		$
		$

BEDROOM #3

		$
		$
		$
		$
		$
		$
		$

BATHROOM

ITEM	PURCHASE DATE	PURCHASE PRICE
		$
		$
		$
		$
		$
		$

GARAGE (include vehicles)

		$
		$
		$
		$
		$
		$

ATTIC

		$
		$
		$
		$
		$
		$

BASEMENT

		$
		$
		$
		$
		$
		$

NAME OF ROOM _____

ITEM	PURCHASE DATE	PURCHASE PRICE
_____	_____	$ _____
_____	_____	$ _____
_____	_____	$ _____
_____	_____	$ _____
_____	_____	$ _____
_____	_____	$ _____

NAME OF ROOM _____

_____	_____	$ _____
_____	_____	$ _____
_____	_____	$ _____
_____	_____	$ _____
_____	_____	$ _____
_____	_____	$ _____

NAME OF ROOM _____

_____	_____	$ _____
_____	_____	$ _____
_____	_____	$ _____
_____	_____	$ _____
_____	_____	$ _____
_____	_____	$ _____

NAME OF ROOM _____

_____	_____	$ _____
_____	_____	$ _____
_____	_____	$ _____
_____	_____	$ _____
_____	_____	$ _____
_____	_____	$ _____

CHECKING ACCOUNTS

BANK

ACCOUNT NUMBER

SAVINGS ACCOUNTS

BANK	ACCOUNT #	DATE	BALANCE
			$
			$
			$
			$
			$
			$
			$
			$
			$
			$
			$
			$
			$
			$
			$
			$
			$
			$
			$

MONEY MARKET FUNDS

FUND_____   Account Number: _____

Date: _____   Balance: _____

Interest Rate: _____   Notes: _____

_____

FUND_____   Account Number: _____

Date: _____   Balance: _____

Interest Rate: _____   Notes: _____

_____

FUND_____   Account Number: _____

Date: _____   Balance: _____

Interest Rate: _____   Notes: _____

_____

FUND_____   Account Number: _____

Date: _____   Balance: _____

Interest Rate: _____   Notes: _____

_____

FUND_____   Account Number: _____

Date: _____   Balance: _____

Interest Rate: _____   Notes: _____

_____

CERTIFICATES OF DEPOSIT

BANK _____   Account Number: _____

Maturity Date: _____   Amount: _____

Interest Rate: _____   Notes: _____

_____

BANK _____   Account Number: _____

Maturity Date: _____   Amount: _____

Interest Rate: _____   Notes: _____

_____

BANK _____   Account Number: _____

Maturity Date: _____   Amount: _____

Interest Rate: _____   Notes: _____

_____

BANK _____   Account Number: _____

Maturity Date: _____   Amount: _____

Interest Rate: _____   Notes: _____

_____

BANK _____   Account Number: _____

Maturity Date: _____   Amount: _____

Interest Rate: _____   Notes: _____

_____

BANK _____   Account Number: _____

Maturity Date: _____   Amount: _____

Interest Rate: _____   Notes: _____

_____

BONDS

SECURITY _____ Number of Bonds: _____

Purchase Price: $ _____ Date Purchased: _____

Current Price & Date: _____

Current Yield & Date: _____

Notes: _____

SECURITY _____ Number of Bonds: _____

Purchase Price: $ _____ Date Purchased: _____

Current Price & Date: _____

Current Yield & Date: _____

Notes: _____

SECURITY _____ Number of Bonds: _____

Purchase Price: $ _____ Date Purchased: _____

Current Price & Date: _____

Current Yield & Date: _____

Notes: _____

SECURITY _____ Number of Bonds: _____

Purchase Price: $ _____ Date Purchased: _____

Current Price & Date: _____

Current Yield & Date: _____

Notes: _____

STOCKS

STOCK _____ Number of Shares: _____

Purchase Price: $ _____ Date Purchased: _____

Current Price & Date: _____

Dividend: _____

Sales Price: $ _____ Date Sold: _____

Notes: _____

STOCK _____ Number of Shares: _____

Purchase Price: $ _____ Date Purchased: _____

Current Price & Date: _____

Dividend: _____

Sales Price: $ _____ Date Sold: _____

Notes: _____

STOCK _____ Number of Shares: _____

Purchase Price: $ _____ Date Purchased: _____

Current Price & Date: _____

Dividend: _____

Sales Price: $ _____ Date Sold: _____

Notes: _____

STOCK _____ Number of Shares: _____

Purchase Price: $ _____ Date Purchased: _____

Current Price & Date: _____

Dividend: _____

Sales Price: $ _____ Date Sold: _____

Notes: _____

MUTUAL FUNDS

FUND_____ Date: _____

Amount of Transaction: $_____ Price Per Share: $_____

Number of Shares Purchased: _____

Number of Shares Redeemed: _____

Total Shares Accumulated: _____

Notes:_____

FUND_____ Date: _____

Amount of Transaction: $_____ Price Per Share: $_____

Number of Shares Purchased: _____

Number of Shares Redeemed: _____

Total Shares Accumulated: _____

Notes:_____

FUND_____ Date: _____

Amount of Transaction: $_____ Price Per Share: $_____

Number of Shares Purchased: _____

Number of Shares Redeemed: _____

Total Shares Accumulated: _____

Notes:_____

FUND_____ Date: _____

Amount of Transaction: $_____ Price Per Share: $_____

Number of Shares Purchased: _____

Number of Shares Redeemed: _____

Total Shares Accumulated: _____

Notes:_____

OTHER SECURITIES

TYPE OF SECURITY: _____ Number:_____

Maturity Date: _____ Amount:_____

Yield of Interest: _____ Notes: _____

TYPE OF SECURITY: _____ Number:_____

Maturity Date: _____ Amount:_____

Yield of Interest: _____ Notes: _____

TYPE OF SECURITY: _____ Number:_____

Maturity Date: _____ Amount:_____

Yield of Interest: _____ Notes: _____

TYPE OF SECURITY: _____ Number:_____

Maturity Date: _____ Amount:_____

Yield of Interest: _____ Notes: _____

TYPE OF SECURITY: _____ Number:_____

Maturity Date: _____ Amount:_____

Yield of Interest: _____ Notes: _____

TYPE OF SECURITY: _____ Number:_____

Maturity Date: _____ Amount:_____

Yield of Interest: _____ Notes: _____

NOTES RECEIVABLE

Indebted Party: _____

Date of Note: _____ Term: _____

Interest: _____ Security: _____

Payment: _____ Call Dates: _____

Notes: _____

_____

_____

Indebted Party: _____

Date of Note: _____ Term: _____

Interest: _____ Security: _____

Payment: _____ Call Dates: _____

Notes: _____

_____

_____

Indebted Party: _____

Date of Note: _____ Term: _____

Interest: _____ Security: _____

Payment: _____ Call Dates: _____

Notes: _____

_____

_____

IRAs

HUSBAND

Company: _____

Current Amount & Date: _____

Current Yield & Date: _____

Notes: _____

Company: _____

Current Amount & Date: _____

Current Yield & Date: _____

Notes: _____

Company: _____

Current Amount & Date: _____

Current Yield & Date: _____

Notes: _____

Company: _____

Current Amount & Date: _____

Current Yield & Date: _____

Notes: _____

IRAs

WIFE

Company: _____

Current Amount & Date: _____

Current Yield & Date: _____

Notes: _____

Company: _____

Current Amount & Date: _____

Current Yield & Date: _____

Notes: _____

Company: _____

Current Amount & Date: _____

Current Yield & Date: _____

Notes: _____

Company: _____

Current Amount & Date: _____

Current Yield & Date: _____

Notes: _____

PENSION OR PROFIT SHARING PLANS

HUSBAND

Employer: _____

Vested Amount & Date: _____

Projected Benefit: _____

Notes: _____

Employer: _____

Vested Amount & Date: _____

Projected Benefit: _____

Notes: _____

Employer: _____

Vested Amount & Date: _____

Projected Benefit: _____

Notes: _____

WIFE

Employer: _____

Vested Amount & Date: _____

Projected Benefit: _____

Notes: _____

Employer: _____

Vested Amount & Date: _____

Projected Benefit: _____

Notes: _____

Employer: _____

Vested Amount & Date: _____

Projected Benefit: _____

Notes: _____

TAX SHELTERED ANNUITY

Owner: _____ Employer: _____

Amount & Date: _____

Current Yield & Date: _____

Notes: _____

Owner: _____ Employer: _____

Amount & Date: _____

Current Yield & Date: _____

Notes: _____

OTHER PLANS

Description: _____

_____

Projected Benefit: _____

Current Amount & Date: _____

Notes: _____

Description: _____

_____

Projected Benefit: _____

Current Amount & Date: _____

Notes: _____

IN CASE OF QUESTIONS ABOUT RETIREMENT PLANS, CALL: _____

_____

_____

_____

_____

PROPERTY — LIABILITY INSURANCE
INCLUDE UMBRELLA POLICIES

Property or Activity Covered: _____

Company: _____ Policy Number: _____

Property: _____ Liability: _____

Living Expense: _____ Deductible: _____

Premium: _____

Property or Activity Covered: _____

Company: _____ Policy Number: _____

Property: _____ Liability: _____

Living Expense: _____ Deductible: _____

Premium: _____

Property or Activity Covered: _____

Company: _____ Policy Number: _____

Property: _____ Liability: _____

Living Expense: _____ Deductible: _____

Premium: _____

Property or Activity Covered: _____

Company: _____ Policy Number: _____

Property: _____ Liability: _____

Living Expense: _____ Deductible: _____

Premium: _____

TOTAL OF PREMIUMS: $ _____

IN CASE OF QUESTIONS ABOUT COVERAGE, CALL: _____

AUTOMOBILE INSURANCE

Vehicle Insured: _____

Company: _____ Policy Number: _____

Comp/Collision: _____ Liability: _____

Deductible: _____ Uninsured Motorist: _____

Premium: _____

Vehicle Insured: _____

Company: _____ Policy Number: _____

Comp/Collision: _____ Liability: _____

Deductible: _____ Uninsured Motorist: _____

Premium: _____

Vehicle Insured: _____

Company: _____ Policy Number: _____

Comp/Collision: _____ Liability: _____

Deductible: _____ Uninsured Motorist: _____

Premium: _____

Vehicle Insured: _____

Company: _____ Policy Number: _____

Comp/Collision: _____ Liability: _____

Deductible: _____ Uninsured Motorist: _____

Premium: _____

HOSPITALIZATION & MEDICAL INSURANCE

Insured: _____

Company: _____ Policy Number: _____

Premium: $_____ Notes: _____

Insured: _____

Company: _____ Policy Number: _____

Premium: $_____ Notes: _____

Insured: _____

Company: _____ Policy Number: _____

Premium: $_____ Notes: _____

Insured: _____

Company: _____ Policy Number: _____

Premium: $_____ Notes: _____

Insured: _____

Company: _____ Policy Number: _____

Premium: $_____ Notes: _____

Insured: _____

Company: _____ Policy Number: _____

Premium: $_____ Notes: _____

Insured: _____

Company: _____ Policy Number: _____

Premium: $_____ Notes: _____

IN CASE OF QUESTIONS ABOUT COVERAGE, CALL: _____

DISABILITY INSURANCE

Insured: _____

Company: _____ Policy Number: _____

Monthly Benefit: $_____ Premium: $_____

Elimination Period: Sickness: _____ Accident: _____

Benefit Period: Sickness: _____ Accident: _____

Residual Benefit: YES ____ NO ____

Inflation Protection: YES ____ NO ____

Insured: _____

Company: _____ Policy Number: _____

Monthly Benefit: $_____ Premium: $_____

Elimination Period: Sickness: _____ Accident: _____

Benefit Period: Sickness: _____ Accident: _____

Residual Benefit: YES ____ NO ____

Inflation Protection: YES ____ NO ____

Insured: _____

Company: _____ Policy Number: _____

Monthly Benefit: $_____ Premium: $_____

Elimination Period: Sickness: _____ Accident: _____

Benefit Period: Sickness: _____ Accident: _____

Residual Benefit: YES ____ NO ____

Inflation Protection: YES ____ NO ____

                                    TOTAL: $_____

IN CASE OF QUESTIONS ABOUT COVERAGE, CALL: _____

LIFE INSURANCE

Insured: _____

Company: _____ Policy Number: _____

Beneficiary: _____

Contingent Beneficiary: _____

Owner: _____ Death Benefit: $ _____

Cash Value: $ _____ Loan: _____

Premium: _____

Insured: _____

Company: _____ Policy Number: _____

Beneficiary: _____

Contingent Beneficiary: _____

Owner: _____ Death Benefit: $ _____

Cash Value: $ _____ Loan: _____

Premium: _____

Insured: _____

Company: _____ Policy Number: _____

Beneficiary: _____

Contingent Beneficiary: _____

Owner: _____ Death Benefit: $ _____

Cash Value: $ _____ Loan: _____

Premium: _____

Insured: _____

Company: _____ Policy Number: _____

Beneficiary: _____

Contingent Beneficiary: _____

Owner: _____ Death Benefit: $_____

Cash Value: $_____ Loan: _____

Premium: _____

Insured: _____

Company: _____ Policy Number: _____

Beneficiary: _____

Contingent Beneficiary: _____

Owner: _____ Death Benefit: $_____

Cash Value: $_____ Loan: _____

Premium: _____

Insured: _____

Company: _____ Policy Number: _____

Beneficiary: _____

Contingent Beneficiary: _____

Owner: _____ Death Benefit: $_____

Cash Value: $_____ Loan: _____

Premium: _____

TOTAL Death Benefits: $_____ Cash Value: $_____

Loans: $_____ Premiums: $_____

MALPRACTICE INSURANCE

Insured: _____

Company: _____ Policy Number: _____

Company Phone: _____ Address: _____

_____

Limits: _____

Premium: _____ Renewal Date: _____

Details: _____

Insured: _____

Company: _____ Policy Number: _____

Company Phone: _____ Address: _____

_____

Limits: _____

Premium: _____ Renewal Date: _____

Details: _____

HOMEOWNER INSURANCE

1. RESIDENCE: _____

Address: _____

Legal Description: _____

Title (Husband, wife, joint, etc.): _____

Date of Purchase: _____ Purchase Price: $_____

Improvements: (Save invoices & cancelled checks)

Date	Improvement	Cost

Current Market Value: _____

Mortgage: _____

Mortgage Balance: _____

2. SECOND RESIDENCE: _____

Address: _____

Legal Description: _____

Title (Husband, wife, joint, etc.): _____

Date of Purchase: _____ Purchase Price: $_____

Improvements: (Save invoices & cancelled checks)

Date	Improvement	Cost

Current Market Value: _____

Mortgage: _____

Mortgage Balance: _____

3. OTHER REAL ESTATE: _____

Address: _____

Legal Description: _____

Title (Husband, wife, joint, etc.): _____

Date of Purchase: _____ Purchase Price: $_____

Improvements: (Save invoices & cancelled checks)

Date	Improvement	Cost

Current Market Value:_____

Mortgage:_____

Mortgage Balance: _____

4. OTHER REAL ESTATE: _____

Address: _____

Legal Description: _____

Title (Husband, wife, joint, etc.): _____

Date of Purchase: _____ Purchase Price: $_____

Improvements: (Save invoices & cancelled checks)

Date	Improvement	Cost

Current Market Value:_____

Mortgage:_____

Mortgage Balance: _____

5. OTHER REAL ESTATE: _____

Address: _____

Legal Description: _____

Title (Husband, wife, joint, etc.): _____

Date of Purchase: _____ Purchase Price: $_____

Improvements: (Save invoices & cancelled checks)

Date	Improvement	Cost

Current Market Value:_____

Mortgage:_____

Mortgage Balance: _____

The Deeds, Mortgages or Deeds of Trust, Title Policies, Abstracts, Surveys, Closing

Statements, Tax Receipts for Improvements, Leases, etc. can be found _____

INDEBTEDNESS

1. MORTGAGES OR DEEDS OF TRUST

a.   Bank: _____

Date of Mortgage: _____

Property: _____

Monthly Payment: $_____ Current Balance: $_____

b.   Bank: _____

Date of Mortgage: _____

Property: _____

Monthly Payment: $_____ Current Balance: $_____

c.   Bank: _____

Date of Mortgage: _____

Property: _____

Monthly Payment: $_____ Current Balance: $_____

d.   Bank: _____

Date of Mortgage: _____

Property: _____

Monthly Payment: $_____ Current Balance: $_____

e.   Bank: _____

Date of Mortgage: _____

Property: _____

Monthly Payment: $_____ Current Balance: $_____

f.   Bank: _____

Date of Mortgage: _____

Property: _____

Monthly Payment: $_____ Current Balance: $_____

INDEBTEDNESS

2. NOTES TO BANKS

a. Bank: _____

Date of Note: _____

Collateral: _____

Monthly Payment: $_____ Current Balance: $_____

b. Bank: _____

Date of Note: _____

Collateral: _____

Monthly Payment: $_____ Current Balance: $_____

c. Bank: _____

Date of Note:_____

Collateral: _____

Monthly Payment: $_____ Current Balance: $_____

3. NOTES TO OTHERS

a. Creditor: _____

Date of Note: _____

Collateral: _____

Monthly Payment: $_____ Current Balance: $_____

4. CREDIT CARDS

a. Credit Card Company: _____

Credit Card Number: _____

Balance: $_____ Monthly Payment: $_____

b. Credit Card Company: _____

Credit Card Number: _____

Balance: $_____ Monthly Payment: $_____

c. Credit Card Company: _____

Credit Card Number: _____

Balance: $_____ Monthly Payment: $_____

5. CAR LOANS

a.   Bank: _____

        Date of Loan: _____ Monthly Payment: $ _____

        Balance: $_____ Collateral: _____

b.   Bank: _____

        Date of Loan: _____ Monthly Payment: $ _____

        Balance: $_____ Collateral: _____

c.   Bank: _____

        Date of Loan: _____ Monthly Payment: $ _____

        Balance: $_____ Collateral: _____

6. OTHER INSTALLMENT LOANS

a.   Creditor: _____ Monthly Payment: $ _____

        Balance: $_____ Collateral: _____

b.   Creditor: _____ Monthly Payment: $ _____

        Balance: $_____ Collateral: _____

c.   Creditor: _____ Monthly Payment: $ _____

        Balance: $_____ Collateral: _____

d.   Creditor: _____ Monthly Payment: $ _____

        Balance: $_____ Collateral: _____

7. ACCOUNTS PAYABLE

a. Creditor: _____

   Balance: $ _____ Monthly Payment: $_____

   Collateral: _____

b. Creditor: _____

   Balance: $ _____ Monthly Payment: $_____

   Collateral: _____

c. Creditor: _____

   Balance: $ _____ Monthly Payment: $_____

   Collateral: _____

8. OTHER LIABILITIES

a. Creditor: _____

   Balance: $ _____ Monthly Payment: $_____

b. Creditor: _____

   Balance: $ _____ Monthly Payment: $_____

c. Creditor: _____

   Balance: $ _____ Monthly Payment: $_____

d. Creditor: _____

   Balance: $ _____ Monthly Payment: $_____

FINANCIAL STATEMENT

ASSETS

	Owner	Value

PERSONAL PROPERTY

Household Items $

Vehicles $

Other $

     $

INVESTMENTS

Checking Accounts $

Savings Accounts $

Money Market Funds $

Certificates of Deposit $

Bonds $

Stocks $

Mutual Funds $

Other Securities $

Cash Value Life Insurance $

RETIREMENT PLANS

IRAs $

Pension or Profit Sharing $

Tax Sheltered Annuities $

REAL ESTATE

Residence $

Investment Properties $

TOTAL ASSETS: $

LIABILITIES

	Owner	Value
Notes Payable to Banks	_____	$ _____
Notes Payable to Others	_____	$ _____
Accounts Payable	_____	$ _____
Credit Cards	_____	$ _____
Mortgage or Residence	_____	$ _____
Other Mortgages	_____	$ _____
Car Loans	_____	$ _____
Installment Loans	_____	$ _____
Other Liabilities:	_____	$ _____

TOTAL LIABILITIES: $ _____

EQUITY: $ _____

SAFETY DEPOSIT BOX INVENTORY

Location: _____ Box Number: _____

Address: _____

Entry Requirements: _____

Contents: _____

_____

_____

_____

_____

_____

_____

_____

_____

_____

_____

_____

_____

_____

_____

_____

_____

_____

_____

_____

_____

_____

_____

_____

_____

_____

FINAL INSTRUCTIONS

(x) Telephone (Check as accomplished)

	Name	Phone
_____ Doctor	_____	_____
_____ Pastor	_____	_____
_____ Hospital for Anatomical Gifts	_____	_____
_____ Funeral Home Place &	_____	_____
& Manner of Internment	_____	_____
_____ Immediate Family	_____	_____
	_____	_____
	_____	_____
	_____	_____
	_____	_____
_____ Close Friends	_____	_____
	_____	_____
	_____	_____
_____ Business Associates	_____	_____
	_____	_____
	_____	_____

_____ Review "Personal Data" in Estate Plan Guide for Death Certificate Accuracy

_____ Make Funeral Arrangements

     _____ If a veteran, take military papers to funeral home.

     _____ Order 5 to 10 Death Certificates through funeral home.

_____ Keep an accurate record of last illness and funeral costs.

_____ Review credit cards — determine if they should be changed or cancelled (see Credit Card list).

_____ Continue to maintain income tax records — you will usually file a joint return in the year of the loss of the spouse.

SPECIAL INSTRUCTIONS

If the decedent was living alone:

_____ Remove important documents and valuables to a safe location.

_____ Notify utility companies and landlord.

_____ Advise post office where to send mail.

Other: _____

_____

_____

_____

_____

APPENDIX B

A. GENERAL

1. How old are you?

20-30	31-40	41-50	51-60	over 60
38	101	64	24	6

2. How old is your spouse?

20-30	31-40	41-50	51-60	over 60
45	85	59	14	5

3. How would you describe your occupation?

professional	vocation or trade	general
233		

4. How will you retire?

full-time	part-time	will not
70	153	9

5. At what age will/did you enter part-time retirement?

30-40	41-50	51-55	56-60	60-62	62-65	65-70	over 70	N/A	directly to FT
1	15	44	46	31	24	26	7	18	12

6. At what age will/did you enter full-time retirement?

30-40	41-50	51-55	56-60	60-62	62-65	65-70	over 70	N/A
	2	10	32	23	24	30	38	62

B. FINANCIAL

1. Your family's approximate annual income is (include all sources of income):

<$20K	$20K-30K	$30-60K	$60-100K	$100-200K	>$200K
4	6	31	60	86	46

2. Your family's current net worth is:

negative	$0	<$25K	$25-50K	$50K-100K	$100-250K	$250-$500K	$500K-1M	$1M-5M	>$5M
36	1	10	14	15	40	28	42	44	2

3. In today's dollars, how much money do you feel you will need to live on annually in retirement?

<$30K	$30-50K	$50-70K	$75-100K	$100-200K	$200-300K	>$300K
1	39	62	81	39	9	

4. What percentage of your current income does this represent?

<50%	50-60%	60-70%	70-80%	80-90%	90-100%	>100%
37	56	26	19	23	36	30

5. What portion of your family's annual income do you save?

none or very little	<2%	2-5%	5-10%	15-20%	20-30%	20-30%	30-40%	>40%
22	18	24	36	58	37	29	5	4

6. In your opinion, what portion of your retirement income will Social Security provide?

0-10%	10-20%	20-30%	30-40%	40-50%	50-60%	60-70%	70-80%	80-90%	90-100%
125	56	30	9	3	2	1	1	1	

7. Do you have a tax-deferred retirement account of any kind?

YES	NO
195	38

8. Do you contribute annually to your tax-deferred retirement account?

YES	NO
174	58

9. How are your assets distributed?

stocks	business value	savings accts & CDs	bonds	cash	real estate	other
39%	35%	19%	23%	13%	36%	29.21%

AVERAGE

10. Are you debt free?

YES	NO
27	206

11. Will you retire debt free?

YES	NO
209	18

C. RETIREMENT LOCATION

1. Where will you retire?

currently live	in/near the ocean/water	in/near mountains	different climate	resort	retirement community	other	town-home	apt. type suite	rent primary residence
129	47	89	20	17	3	2	10		

2. In retirement, our housing plans include:

same home	upsize to larger	buy pre-built	condo	time share	downsize to smaller	build new	town-home	apt. type suite	rent primary residence
106	5	9	34	12	72	41	11	2	3

3. If you plan to retire, either part-time or full-time, into a home other than your current residence, do you plan to purchase that home before retirement?

YES	NO	N/A

4. Will your children or other family members affect your decision as to where you will retire?

YES	NO	N/A
126	29	66

If so, who will affect that decision?

	very much	somewhat	very little
If so, who will affect that decision?	151	63	18
a. Children	97	54	12
b. Parents &/or Grandparents	18	70	70
c. Close Friends	8	99	55

5. How would you rate your retirement plans as a couple?

agree closely on almost all issues	general agreement on most issues	significantly different retirement ideas	N/A
91	105	4	30

6. As a couple, how much time have you and your spouse spent planning retirement?

frequently discuss	discussed most major issues	need to spend much more time on it	hardly ever discuss	N/A
25	71	61	51	26

D. HEALTH & WELLNESS

	YES	NO
1. Is current failing health or inability to perform your work a factor in deciding when or how you will retire?	17	215
2. Do you feel you will enter retirement in good health?	226	6
3. Do you smoke?	10	224
4. Do you consume excess alcohol?	6	227

5. How would you rate your lifestyle in the following areas?

	excellent	good	average	fair	poor
a. Diet	39	114	56	17	7
b. Exercise	47	81	55	37	13
c. Rest	26	86	84	31	6
d. Preventive Care	71	112	39	11	
e. Psychological Health	105	98	25	4	1

6. How much do the following health issues concern you as you age?

	very much	somewhat	very little
a. Heart related conditions	39	108	82
b. Cancer	32	102	96
c. Stroke	16	89	125
d. Alzheimer's or other dementia	17	70	143
e. Musculoskeletal problem	33	110	87
f. Other: RA Family History		1	
g. Other: Diabetes	2	7	
h. Other: Osteoporosis		1	
i. Other: High Blood Pressure	1	1	
j. Other: Liver		1	
k. Other: Prostate Cancer		1	

E. INSURANCE & ASSET PROTECTION

	none	<$100K	$100-300K	$300-500K	$500K-1M	$1M-3M	>$3M
1. How much life insurance do you (or the major wage earner) have?							

	21	8	70	40	56	34	3
2. Do you have disability insurance?	**YES** 129	**NO** 102					
If so, how much per month?	**<$1K** 6	**$1-2K** 12	**$2-3K** 26	**$3-5K** 48	**$5-10K** 34	**>$10K** 2	
3. Do you have long-term care insurance?	**YES** 27	**NO** 205					
If no, do you plan to get it at a later date?	**YES** 97	**NO** 81					
4. Do you have a will?	141	90					
5. Do you maintain, in a single location & good order, all information needed to settle your estate?	120	110					
6. Do you have the following asset protection vehicles in place?							
a. Holding Assets in Joint Tenancy (w/right of survivor)	107	125					
b. Corporations & LLCs	90	139					
c. Trusts	63	168					
d. Family Limited Partnerships	28	201					
e. International Asset Protection Trust	6	224					

ABOUT THE AUTHOR

David Kats was born on a Nebraska farm in the early baby boomer years. He received his Bachelor's Degree from the University of Nebraska and Doctor of Chiropractic Degree from Palmer College of Chiropractic. During the first half of his professional career, he built one of the largest chiropractic practices in the United States. In 1989, he was voted Chiropractor of the Year by the American Chiropractic Association. He has also served on the Nebraska State Board of Health. Dr. Kats and his partner, Keith Maule, now own the nation's largest chiropractic business consulting firm. He and his wife, Linda, have homes in Nebraska, Oklahoma, and Florida.

INDEX

M8048-D
99 TN